At Issue

How Can Gang Violence Be Prevented?

Other books in the At Issue series:

At Issue

How Can Gang Violence Be Prevented?

Christi Watkins, Book Editor

GREENHAVEN PRESS

An imprint of Thomson Gale, a part of The Thomson Corporation

THOMSON

™

GALE

Detroit • New York • San Francisco • New Haven, Conn. • Waterville, Maine • London

THOMSON

✳ ™

GALE

Christine Nasso, *Publisher*
Elizabeth Des Chenes, *Managing Editor*

© 2007 Thomson Gale, a part of The Thomson Corporation.

Thomson and Star Logo are trademarks and Gale and Greenhaven Press are registered trademarks used herein under license.

For more information, contact:
Greenhaven Press
27500 Drake Rd.
Farmington Hills, MI 48331-3535
Or you can visit our Internet site at http://www.gale.com

LIBRARY OF CONGRESS CATALOGING-IN-PUBLICATION DATA

How can gang violence be prevented? / Christi Watkins, book editor.
   p. cm. -- (At issue)
Includes bibliographical references and index.
ISBN-13: 978-0-7377-2380-9 (lib. : alk. paper)
ISBN-10: 0-7377-2380-7 (lib. : alk. paper)
ISBN-13: 978-0-7377-2381-6 (pbk. : alk. paper)
ISBN-10: 0-7377-2381-5 (pbk. : alk. paper)
1. Gangs--United States--Juvenile literature. 2. Juvenile delinquency--United States--Prevention--Juvenile literature. 3. Violent crimes--United States--Prevention--Juvenile literature. 4. Violence--United States--Prevention--Juvenile literature. I. Watkins, Christine, 1951–
   HV6439.U5H678 2007
   364.40973--dc22
                                                        2006022932

Printed in the United States of America
10 9 8 7 6 5 4 3 2 1

Contents

Introduction

In 2003 a pregnant seventeen-year-old girl was stabbed sixteen times by members of the Mara Salvatrucha gang and left to die on the banks of the Shenandoah River in Virginia. In May 2006 on a street filled with children in San Bernardino, California, a thirteen-year-old boy was killed by a gang member who shot indiscriminately into a group of people standing in a driveway. In the same month in Fort Worth, Texas, thirteen-year-old Sammy Stevenson was headed home after swimming when he was caught in the middle of gunfire between rival gangs. He would have graduated from middle school two days later. In small towns as well as large cities across the United States, over twenty thousand gangs with more than seven hundred thousand gang members have established a presence. Many of these gangs are involved in drug dealing, prostitution, the sale of illegal weapons, assault, and murder, and many innocent people are becoming the victims of gang violence.

Experts agree that criminal gangs have become highly organized and are growing more rapidly and more violent than ever before. Wesley McBride, former Los Angeles County sheriff and former president of the National Alliance of Gang Investigators Association, told the U.S. Senate Committee on the Judiciary in September 2003, "The malignancy of the gang presence kills communities just as surely as their bullets kill people. . . . Their ability to instill fear into the people of a community knows no bounds. They will kill indiscriminately to make their point." Although most law enforcement officers, government leaders, and citizens agree that gang violence is a serious national problem, there is a serious debate over the best approach to preventing it. Some believe that much stronger law enforcement and criminal penalties—a tough-on-crime approach—is most effective. Others disagree, arguing that the reason young people join gangs is a lack of support, guidance, and encouragement in their families and schools. They believe that more community outreach programs are needed to prevent the problem of gang violence.

One law enforcement officer who believes in the tough-on-crime approach is Los Angeles police chief William Bratton. As police commissioner of New York City from 1994 to 1996, he greatly increased the number of police officers on the streets and the number of criminals in jail, resulting in a 50 percent drop in the homicide rate in that city. After he became the Los Angeles police chief in 2002 he again cracked down on crime, enlisting the help of federal law enforcement agencies such as the FBI and the Drug Enforcement Administration. As a result, the homicide rate in the most violent, gang-ridden area of Los Angeles—the Seventy-seventh Division, five miles south of downtown—dropped by 45 percent in his first year as police chief. Bratton insists, "The penicillin for dealing with crime is cops." Helen Coleman, a community member of the Seventy-seventh Division, agrees with Bratton's approach, arguing that stricter enforcement makes citizens feel safer. As she told writer Terry McCarthy for an article in *Time* magazine, "There has to be hope in a community, and I think we have that now."

Some leaders in the federal government also want to make ending gang violence a priority, and they tackle it in much the same way as the government confronts organized crime and terrorism—through increased legislation and law enforcement. U.S. senator from California Dianne Feinstein has introduced the Gang Prevention and Effective Deterrence Act of 2005 (S.155), and Virginia congressman James Randy Forbes has sponsored the Gang Deterrence and Community Protection Act of 2005 (H.R.1279), both of which demand larger and more powerful police forces and antigang units, as well as the prosecution of juvenile gang members as adults and harsher prison sentences for convicted gang members. Congressman Forbes told the members of a legislative hearing, "Gangs have declared war on our nation. They are ravaging our communities like cancer—urban, rural, rich, and poor—and they are metastasizing from one community to the next as they grow. With the introduction of the 'gangbusters' legislation, we declare war on gangs."

Many other researchers and community leaders, however, believe that creating more stringent laws and increasing law enforcement efforts does not and will not prevent gang violence. Tom Hayden, a former California state senator and assemblyman representing Los Angeles, wrote in his book *Street Wars: Gangs and the Future of Violence* that "after three decades of thundering law-and-order rhetoric from politicians, police, and prison officials, it is time to recognize that the war on gangs has become a bloody quagmire with no end in sight. We are tougher on crime than any comparable nation in the world, measured by arrests, incarcerations, and police and prison expenditures. And yet the crisis deepens."

Author Jens Soering, who is serving two life sentences for a double murder, argues that increasing the prosecution of juvenile delinquents will not prevent gang violence. Writing in the March 21, 2005, issue of *America* magazine, Soering states, "Unfortunately, at-risk youths do not enjoy being bullied any more than anyone else does, and they respond to being menaced by becoming more menacing themselves."

Indeed, researchers and community leaders insist that to effectively reduce gang violence, young people must be offered alternatives and opportunities that will prevent them from joining gangs in the first place. Early intervention in a child's life is essential. Many gang members are kids who have not succeeded in school (80 percent have learning disabilities), have nothing to do with their time, do not feel good about themselves, and believe they do not have anything to look forward to. Children and teenagers often view gangs as extended families that provide protection, identification, status, and acceptance. They feel that they have nothing to lose if they go to jail.

Community prevention and intervention programs offer at-risk youth an opportunity to develop healthy interests and friendships and can provide caring adults and other positive role models when families are unavailable. Programs that enable young people to find employment or that provide educational support such as tutoring are vital in building adolescents' self-esteem—and decrease the likelihood that they will become involved in gang activity, some community activists argue. In his 2005 State of the Union Address, President George W. Bush noted, "We need to focus on giving young people, especially young men in our cities, better options than apathy, or gangs, or jail."

The controversy over increasing criminal penalties for gang members and developing more community outreach programs for youth is just one of many debates over how to prevent gang violence. In *At Issue: How Can Gang Violence Be Prevented?* the authors present a variety of perspectives on what leads to gang membership and the measures proposed to combat the growing problem of gang violence, including stricter deportation laws, closing the U.S. borders, and mandatory school uniforms.

1

Federal Legislation Against Gang Members Will Prevent Gang Violence

Dianne Feinstein

Dianne Feinstein is a Democratic U.S. senator from California.

The number of street gangs in the United States has dramatically escalated, and approximately 840,000 gang members now pose a growing national public safety threat. Every state of the Union is affected by gang violence, which includes murder, kidnapping, robbery, and drug dealing. The United States must therefore develop a national strategy to provide federal, state, and local law enforcement the tools needed to attack this problem of gang violence. The Gang Prevention and Effective Deterrence Act of 2005 would provide those tools. This comprehensive bill defines and criminalizes violent acts in furtherance or in aid of criminal street gangs, supports witness protection programs, and funds intervention and prevention programs for at-risk youth. This bill is a tough but fair solution to the problem of gang violence.

Criminal street gangs have grown over the past two decades from a local problem to a national crisis. Every day, we read about a new tragedy—where a gang member has shot a police officer as part of an induction ceremony, used a machete to murder an innocent victim, or tracked down and killed someone who may have witnessed a crime. There are

Dianne Feinstein, remarks made at a Field Hearing by the U.S. Senate Judiciary Committee at the National Constitution Center in Philadelphia, Pennsylvania, June 13, 2005.

reports of gangs actively recruiting elementary school students—7 and 8 years old—into their criminal enterprise. They must be stopped.

The Extent of Gang Violence

I would like to take a moment to outline the magnitude of the problem.

- It is estimated that there are 840,000 active gang members in the U.S., operating in every state of the Union.

- 90% of large cities (with a population of over 100,000) report gang activity, and that is not the full extent of the problem. In 2002, 32% of cities with a population of 25 [thousand] to 50 thousand reported a gang-related homicide.

- In California, the most recent statistics available indicate that between 1992 and 2003, 7851 people were killed in gang-related violence. In the first quarter of 2005, Los Angeles County alone reported 1727 gang crimes.

- In 2003, there were 115 gangland murders, and 819 juvenile gang killings.

In other words, youth gangs killed seven times as many people as so-called organized crime. In fact, many street gangs are now highly organized, hierarchical "corporations," with boards of directors, governors and regional coordinators.

As Los Angeles Chief of Police, William Bratton, has said, "There is nothing more insidious than these gangs. They are worse than the Mafia. Show me a year in New York where the Mafia indiscriminately killed 300 people. You can't."

Strong Preventive Tactics

In recognition of this emerging threat, the FBI [in May 2005] formed a nationwide taskforce to disrupt the organization of the notorious MS-13. This single gang operates in at least 33 states, with an international membership in the hundreds of thousands. On Christmas Eve 2004, MS-13 members gunned down 28 commuters on a passenger bus in Honduras. The mastermind of that attack was arrested in Texas in February. This same gang is responsible for the brutal murder of a 17-year-old informant in Virginia. She was four months pregnant and stabbed 16 times in the chest and neck. I need not remind my colleagues of the wave of machete attacks perpetrated by MS-13 in the Washington, D.C. area.

Just as the RICO [Racketeer Influenced and Corrupt Organizations] Act was needed to break up mafia rings, I believe federal and local law enforcement need a strong set of tools to combat violent gangs today.

With my distinguished colleagues Senators [Orrin] Hatch, [Charles] Grassley, [Jon] Kyl and [John] Cornyn, I have introduced S.155, "The Gang Prevention and Effective Deterrence Act of 2005."

Its main point is to create a new type of crime, by defining and criminalizing "criminal street gangs." This recognizes the basic point of a street gang—it is more powerful, and more dangerous, than its individual members. Defeating gangs means recognizing what is so dangerous about them, and then making that conduct against the law.

This bill does exactly that.

First, it makes participation in a criminal street gang a federal crime. A "criminal street gang" is defined to mean a formal or informal group, club, organization or association of 3 or more persons who act together to commit gang crimes.

This legislation makes it a crime for a member of a criminal street gang to commit, conspire or attempt to commit two or more predicate gang crimes; or to get another individual to commit a gang crime;

The term "gang crime" is defined to include violent and other serious State and Federal felony crimes such as: murder, maiming, manslaughter, kidnapping, arson, robbery, assault with a dangerous weapon, obstruction of justice, carjacking, distribution of a controlled substance, certain firearms offenses and money laundering. And it criminalizes violent crimes in furtherance or in aid of criminal street gangs.

These two provisions are at the heart of this legislation. Armed with this new law, Federal prosecutors, working in tandem with State and local law enforcement, will be able to take on gangs in much the same way that traditional Mafia families have been systematically destroyed by effective RICO prosecutions. The legislation also recognizes that the core changes, standing alone, are not sufficient.

The Gang Prevention and Effective Deterrence Act is a comprehensive bill to increase gang prosecution and prevention efforts. The bill authorizes approximately $750 million [from 2005–2010] to support Federal, State and local law enforcement efforts against violent gangs, including the funding of witness protection programs and for intervention and prevention programs for at-risk youth. In support of this effort, the bill increases funding for Federal prosecutors and FBI agents to increase coordinated enforcement efforts against violent gangs.

We have to keep our children and grandchildren out of violent gangs.

Protection for the Community

In addition to enforcement, we must encourage a community response to the gang problem. Gang members are increasingly seeking to silence those who step forward to incriminate them. Routine witness intimidation has given way to routine witness execution. As an example, recent press reports from Boston show that gang members are distributing what is, in essence, a witness intimidation media kit, complete with graphics and CDs that warn potential witnesses that they will be killed—

one CD depicts three bodies on its covers. In another incident, a witness's grand jury testimony was taped to his home—soon afterward he was killed. I believe it is vital to support those who speak out against the violence in their communities, and this bill provides $60 million to create and expand witness protection programs.

Most important of all, we have to keep our children and grandchildren out of violent gangs. We must identify and fund successful community programs that stem gang recruitment and participation. Today we will learn from those on the front lines in the effort to combat gang and youth violence how best to approach this issue. What works, what does not work, and how to combine effective law enforcement tools with workable prevention mechanisms. This bill authorizes $250 million to make grants available for community-based programs to provide for crime prevention and intervention services for gang members and at-risk youth in areas designated as high intensity interstate gang activity areas. We must ensure that this funding is used wisely.

The bottom line is that this legislation would provide the tools and the resources to begin the national task of destroying criminal street gangs. It is designed to emphasize and encourage Federal, State and local cooperation. It combines enforcement with prevention. It is a tough, effective and fair approach. . . .

We all agree that gangs are a terrible and growing problem. We all agree that something needs to be done. I believe that this legislation is desperately needed, and I look forward to working with my colleagues on both sides of the aisle to take this bill and make it law. . . .

A Summary of the Bill

The "Gang Prevention and Effective Deterrence Act of 2005," is a comprehensive criminal bill to increase gang prosecution *and* prevention efforts. The bill:

- Authorizes $400 million [from 2005–2010] to support Federal, State and local law enforcement efforts against violent gangs, including witness protection programs;

- Authorizes an additional $350 million over the [same] five years for intervention and prevention programs for at-risk youth;

- Increases funding for federal prosecutors and FBI agents to increase coordinated enforcement efforts against violent gangs;

- Creates a new, RICO-like anti-gang section to penalize those who commit or conspire to commit crimes in furtherance of a criminal gang.

- Creates new criminal gang prosecution offenses to prohibit recruitment of minors in[to] a criminal street gang, and to punish violent crimes related to gangs;

- Increases penalties for existing gang and violent crimes to deter and punish illegal street gangs, and proposes violent crime reforms needed to effectively prosecute gang members;

- Creates a new High Intensity Interstate Gang Activity Area program to facilitate cooperation between local, state and federal law enforcement in identifying, targeting, and eliminating violent gangs in areas where gang activity is particularly prevalent; and

- Enacts a limited reform of the juvenile justice system with judicial oversight to facilitate federal prosecution of 16- and 17-year-old gang members who commit serious acts of violence.

2

Federal Legislation Against Gang Members Will Not Prevent Gang Violence

American Civil Liberties Union

The American Civil Liberties Union is a national organization that works to defend Americans' civil rights as guaranteed by the U.S. Constitution.

Although gang violence is a serious problem in the United States, the federal gang legislation that California senator Dianne Feinstein has introduced is not the solution. The Gang Prevention and Effective Deterrence Act (S.155) would make several gang-related offenses punishable by the death penalty. It is wrong to expand the use of the death penalty, a system which is in need of reform rather than expansion. This bill would also permit prosecutors to charge nonviolent offenders with gang crimes, even if they are not members of a gang. Furthermore, under S.155, children could be tried as adults and incarcerated in adult prisons, a practice which turns children into hardened criminals. This legislation against gang members will not prevent gang violence and should not be enacted into law.

Senator Feinstein (D-CA) has introduced S.155, the Gang Prevention and Effective Deterrence Act of 2005 ("Gang bill"). The Gang bill would subject innocent people to the death penalty, creates a very broad and vague definition of a

American Civil Liberties Union, "Greg Nojeim and Jesselyn McCurdy's Letter to Senators Specter and Leahy Urging Opposition of S.155, Gang Prevention and Deterrence Act of 2005," June 30, 2005. Copyright © 2005 ACLU, 125 Broad Street, 18th floor, New York, NY 10004. Reproduced by permission.

"gang," makes nearly every major federal crime involving three or more people a "gang" crime, results in wrongful convictions based on unreliable evidence, and creates more serious juvenile offenders by incarcerating children in adult prisons. . . .

The Death Penalty Should Not Be Expanded

Expansion of the federal death penalty undermines the very reforms that were enacted in [2004's] Justice for All Act (P.L. 108-405), which addressed some systemic problems with the federal death penalty. S.155 would create several new gang related offenses and make them punishable by the death penalty as well as increase the penalty for an existing offense to the possibility of a death sentence. The death penalty is in need of reform, not expansion. According to the Death Penalty Information Center, 119 prisoners on death row have now been exonerated. Chronic problems, including inadequate defense counsel and racial disparities, plague the death penalty system in the United States. The expansion of the death penalty potential for gang crimes creates an opportunity for more arbitrary application of the death penalty. States continue to address the systemic problems with the administration of the death penalty by implementing reform and moratorium efforts, while the federal government, in S.155, is moving to expand the death penalty in lieu of enacting or implementing reforms on the federal level.

In addition to expanding the number of federal death penalty crimes, the bill expands venue in capital cases to the point that any location even tangentially related to the crime could be the site of a trial. This raises constitutional as well as public policy concerns. The Constitution states that "the Trial of all Crimes . . . shall be by Jury; and shall be held in the State where the said Crimes shall have been committed." Prosecuting cases in the jurisdiction where the crime occurred is important in order to prevent undue hardship and unfairness when an accused person is prosecuted in a place that has no significant connection to the offense with which he is charged. Studies of the federal death penalty show that a person prosecuted in Texas is much more likely to be charged, tried and sentenced to death in a capital case than a person who is prosecuted for the same crime in Massachusetts. This bill will exacerbate these geographic inequities that exist in the federal death penalty system. The wide range of discretion in both what to charge and where to bring the charge will give prosecutors tremendous latitude to forum shop. This broad discretion will increase the racial and geographic disparities already at play in the federal death penalty.

This bill would impose severe penalties for a collective group of three or more people who commit non-violent offenses. Title I revises the already broad definition of "criminal street gang" to an even more ambiguous standard of "a formal or informal group, club or organization of three (3) or more people who individually, jointly, or in combination have committed or attempted to commit" at least two (2) predicate gang crimes for the benefit or furtherance of the "gang" within 10 years of each other. The informal group or associates of three or more people must commit one predicate crime of violence or a drug trafficking crime that affects interstate commerce to qualify as a gang.

People who may commit a non-violent offense could be considered gang members.

Innocent People Could Be Convicted of a "Gang" Crime

The number of people required to form a gang decreases from five (5) people in an ongoing group under current law to three (3) people who could be just associates or casual acquaintances under this proposed legislation. Under the Gang bill a "continuing series" of crimes do not have to be established to charge a person with a gang crime. Presently, the government has to establish that criminal street gangs engaged "within the past five (5) years in a continuing series of offenses." The continuing series of offenses under current law is essential to preserving the concept of gang activity that the law is trying to target; i.e. criminal activity that has some type of connection to a tight knit group of people. S.155 would permit prosecutors to charge non-violent offenders with gang crimes. The prosecutor is only required to prove that two (2) or more predicate gang offenses were committed within 10 years of each other (excluding any time served in jail or prison). This provision would result in people being convicted of "gang" crimes that have no ongoing nature and that have no connection to each other that occurred 10 years or more apart.

Predicate gang crimes consist of virtually every major federal offense, including gambling and burglary. Any conspiracy to commit a predicate gang offense would also qualify as a predicate offense. Under this legislation's definition of a criminal street gang, people who may commit a non-violent offense could be considered gang members. For example, if a person is with two friends who attempt to sell drugs to an undercover officer and any of the three later provide police with a false identification the person who was not involved in the attempted drug transaction will still be responsible [for] both gang crimes. Even though the person never participated in the attempted drug deal and was not a member of a "gang," he would go to prison for committing a gang crime.

The Right to a Fair Trial Could Be Jeopardized

Innocent people could be convicted of crimes they did not commit if the statute of limitations is extended as proposed in this legislation. Title II of the Gang bill would extend the statute of limitations for non-capital crimes of violence. Generally, the statute of limitations for non-capital federal crimes is five (5) years after the offense is committed. This bill would extend that limitation for crimes of violence to 10 years after the offense was committed or the continuing offense was completed, or eight (8) years after the offense was discovered. For example, if a violent crime was committed in 2004, but it wasn't discovered until 2014 the statute of limitations would be extended until 2022. In 2022, 18 years after the crime, alibi witnesses could have disappeared or died, other witnesses' memories would have faded and evidence may be unreliable. This could affect a person's ability to defend themselves against charges and to receive a fair trial if older evidence and less re-liable witness testimony are used against them during a trial.

More children will become hardened criminals after be-ing . . . incarcerated in adult prisons.

In addition, shifting the burden of proof for pretrial de-tention in some cases involving guns could result in serious injustices and interfere with an accused person's defense. This legislation would create a rebuttal presumption against bail for people accused of certain firearms offenses during the commission of serious drug crimes. A person who is pre-sumed innocent and has not been found guilty of any crime could be held for months or years without the government having made any showing that he or she is dangerous or a flight risk. Making it more difficult for an accused person to be released on bail prior to trial hinders a defendant's ability to assist the person's defense lawyer with investigating the facts of the case and preparing their defense.

Juveniles Could Be Harmed

Under the Gang bill, more children will become hardened criminals after being tried in federal court and incarcerated in adult prisons. Currently under federal law, when the government recommends trying a juvenile as an adult in federal court various factors must be considered by the court before deciding whether the criminal prosecution of a young person is in the interest of justice. These factors include the age, social background, and the intellectual development and psychological maturity of the child. S.155 would permit the prosecutor the discretion to determine when to try a young person in federal court as an adult, if the juvenile is 16 years of age or older, commits a crime of violence and has a prior juvenile adjudication (that would have been a serious felony) and commits a subsequent felony involving physical force in relation to drug trafficking or smuggling, arson, or destruction of an aircraft or vessel. A child 16 years or older who commits a serious violent felony will also be subjected to prosecution in adult criminal court. The only recourse that the young person will have is to attempt to persuade the court during a "reverse waiver" hearing that he should not be tried as an adult and sent to adult prison. This legislation shifts the burden squarely on the shoulders of the child to overcome a presumption that the child should be prosecuted in adult court and establish by clear and convincing evidence that it would be in the interest of justice that he be tried in juvenile court.

The federal system does not have the resources or the facilities to address the needs of youth under the age of 18. The federal government should continue to let states deal with juveniles in their family court systems that were created to address the needs and provide services to young people. A 1996 study showed that youth transferred to adult court in Florida were a third more likely to reoffend than those sent to the juvenile justice system for the same crime and with similar prior records. Of the youth in this study who committed new crimes, those sent to adult court reoffended at twice the rate of those sent to juvenile court. This research emphasizes the need for juveniles to be held accountable in the juvenile justice system, which has more resources to address the problems that cause children to come to the attention of the court system.

While efforts to address gang crime are very important to maintaining public safety, this legislation proposes to confront crime at the expense of the right to a fair trial, at the risk of convicting innocent people and unnecessary exposure to the death penalty. S.155 will not solve the problem of gang crime in this country, thus senators should oppose this bill when it is considered by the Senate Judiciary Committee.

3

Deportation Laws Will Decrease Gang Violence

Kris W. Kobach

Kris W. Kobach is a professor of law at the University of Missouri–Kansas City.

Street gangs of illegal aliens, responsible for hundreds of murders in the United States, present a deadly threat and a difficult challenge to law enforcement agencies. To combat this problem, the United States should strengthen immigration laws and deport illegal aliens who are known to be affiliated with violent gangs, even before they commit a crime. Furthermore, U.S. law enforcement officers should seize all property used by alien gang members during the commission of their crimes as well as assets obtained from their crimes. Deportation and forfeiture of assets would have a strong impact in reducing gang violence.

The alien street gangs that are responsible for hundreds of murders in the United States in the last few years present an extremely difficult law enforcement challenge. As one police officer told me recently, these gangs present a far more deadly threat than their predecessors. Compared to the dominant gangs of the early 1990s, which were composed primarily of U.S. citizens from inner-city areas, today's street gangs are composed overwhelmingly of illegal aliens and are more vio-

Kris W. Kobach, prepared statement before the Subcommittee on Immigration, Border Security and Claims, legislative hearing regarding H.R. 2933, the Alien Gang Removal Act, before the U.S. House of Representatives Committee on the Judiciary, 109th Congress, http://judiciary.house.gov, June 28, 2005.

lent, more likely to kill, and more likely to operate within well-organized criminal networks that not only span the country, but span the continent.

The Scope of the Problem

A few statistics illustrate the scope of the problem. Mara Salvatrucha-13 (MS-13), the most notorious and fastest-growing alien gang, started as a Salvadoran gang in Los Angeles in the late 1980s. Its association with El Salvador has always been an important part of its identity, with gang members in many cities using the blue and white national colors of El Salvador as their gang colors. MS-13's more than 10,000 members operate in at least 33 states. Those states are as far flung as Alaska, Michigan, Idaho, Georgia, New York, and Nebraska. The overwhelming majority of its members are illegal aliens, primarily from El Salvador, but also from Honduras. The presence of MS-13 is particularly strong in the metropolitan Washington, D.C., area (including northern Virginia and southern Maryland), with an estimated 5,000 to 6,000 members. But MS-13 also has established a very large footprint in areas that have not previously been subject to gang violence. There are approximately 200 MS-13 members in Charlotte, North Carolina. There are approximately 300 in suburban Long Island. And MS-13 still remains smaller than the largest alien gang, the 18th Street Gang—which started in Los Angeles with primarily Mexican membership and then expanded nationwide. It is estimated to have more than 20,000 members in the Los Angeles area alone. In both gangs, the majority of members are *illegal* aliens. The gangs generate cash in different ways in different parts of the country. But by far, the most common forms of activity are drug trafficking, theft, gun trafficking and immigrant smuggling.

Where MS-13 or the 18th Street Gang establish a presence, the blood inevitably flows soon thereafter. In Los Angeles, the various street gangs accounted for 291 of the city's 515 homicides in 2004—an increase of 12.4% in gang killings over 2003. In places newly acquainted with alien gang activity, the numbers are smaller, but each murder is more shocking to these once gang-free communities. In Charlotte, for example, MS-13 members have committed at least 19 murders in the three years between 2000 and 2003.

Consider the example of Omaha, Nebraska, not far from where I live. Mid-sized Midwestern cities like Omaha have recently seen the growth of illegal alien gangs—an entirely new phenomenon for local law enforcement. Omaha is a city that typically sees between 20 and 30 homicides a year. However, in late 2004, there was a dramatic increase in violence in south Omaha, perpetrated mainly by alien gangs. MS-13 and the 18th Street Gang increased their presence in the city, and this is reflected in recent statistics. According to the Omaha Police Department figures, total gang activity in the fourth quarter of 2004 increased 27% (over the same period the previous year), and gang activity in the first quarter of 2005 increased 39%. The number of homicides has risen accordingly, with the increase almost entirely attributable to the gangs.

The alien gangs in Omaha control and perpetuate the drug trade there. According to the National Drug Intelligence Center, the marijuana in Omaha comes primarily from Mexican criminal gangs who transport it into the state by road using private and commercial vehicles. The same is true of the powdered and crack cocaine distributed in Omaha. And contrary to popular misconception, the majority of methamphetamine in Omaha comes from Mexico or California through the alien gang network. Although methamphetamine can be produced virtually anywhere, the alien gangs dominate the trade, bringing it in from south of the border or from California. This once-quiet city now hears the gunfire of alien street gangs with disturbing regularity.

Extradition Barriers

Gangs composed primarily of aliens possess an advantage over law enforcement that other gangs do not have—sanctuaries in foreign countries that refuse to extradite criminals eligible for the death penalty. Those countries include Mexico and El Salvador. Mexico is the most notorious example, with more than 3,000 individuals who are suspected of committing murder in the United States now at large in their home country of Mexico. Mexico has no formal extradition arrangement with the United States. And since the Mexican Supreme Court's ruling in October 2001 (that life imprisonment is unconstitutional), that country has also resisted extraditing criminal suspects who are eligible for life imprisonment if convicted. El Salvador's constitution currently bans the extradition of Salvadoran nationals.

This not only creates a sanctuary for gang members after they have committed their crimes in the United States, it may also be contributing to a disturbing incentive for gang members operating in the United States. The frequency of execution-style murders carried out by MS-13, the 18th Street Gang, and other gangs has been widely reported. Many in the law enforcement community will tell you that some alien gang members have intentionally and deliberately shot to kill, including shooting wounded victims through the head. One prominent theory is that many alien gang members do this in order to make sure that their crime is first degree murder—serious enough to bar extradition. Establishing the motive of such killers with certainty is obviously problematic. But given gang members' frequent reliance on the absence of extradition arrangements in order to evade U.S. law enforcement, it is not at all unreasonable to suspect that many intentionally heighten the severity of their crimes.

The Use of Immigration Enforcement

Because so many of these gang members are aliens without lawful presence in the United States, sustained and focused enforcement efforts by Immigration and Customs Enforcement (ICE) can have a massive impact in fighting this national scourge. This was perhaps most dramatically demonstrated in March 2005, when ICE announced the arrest of 103 members of MS-13 in an operation spanning several weeks. Known as Operation Community Shield, it led to the arrest of 30 gang members in New York, 25 in the Washington, D.C., area, 17 in Los Angeles, 10 in Newark, and 10 in Miami. Although all were arrested for violations of federal immigration laws, approximately half had prior arrest records or prior convictions for violent crimes.

Immigration enforcement can serve to remove illegal aliens who pose a danger to the community due to their membership in violent gangs.

This successful ICE operation was accomplished through the sharing of information between state and local law enforcement. Local police departments provided to ICE lists of names that those police departments had compiled of known alien gang members. ICE was then able to run that list through its databases to determine which, if any of those aliens was legally present in the country. After determining that the alien gang members were illegally present, ICE moved in with a series of arrests.

Operation Community Shield was not the first use of immigration law enforcement against these gangs. In October–November 2004, ICE agents worked with local law enforcement in San Diego to arrest 45 MS-13 members. And in 2003, ICE worked with local law enforcement in Charlotte to arrest and remove more than 100 MS-13 gang members.

This episode demonstrates well how focusing immigration enforcement efforts against particular immigration violators can provide invaluable support to local law enforcement in their efforts to stem gang violence. It is an undeniable fact that immigration enforcement is a tool that can be used to effectively combat gangs when illegal aliens comprise a substantial proportion of gang members. Just as many members of terrorist organizations were removed after 9/11 on immigration violations rather than being prosecuted in criminal courts, so too immigration enforcement can serve to remove illegal aliens who pose a danger to the community due to their membership in violent gangs. . . .

Civil Forfeiture of Assets

A basic problem with the use of removal proceedings against these gang members is that so many of them return to the country with impunity after being removed. The immense problem of prior deportees returning to the United States can be seen in the thousands upon thousands of reinstatements of prior removal orders and encounters of prior deportees by federal immigration enforcement officers. It is an undeniable fact that many of these career criminals move back and forth across our borders with impunity. The threat of being removed again is simply no deterrent whatsoever for these individuals.

> *[Illegal alien gang members] not only have no right to prey upon our society, they have no right to the proceeds of their violent and destructive activity.*

Civil forfeiture of assets would change the calculation substantially. If an alien gang member knew that there was a high probability that law enforcement officers could seize all property used in his criminal gang activity, including his automobile, any equipment used in the commission of his crimes, and the proceeds of his crimes, he would have substantial reason to relocate his gang activities outside of the United States and remain there. The risk of facing civil forfeiture would dramatically increase the cost of returning to the US to "do business."

Judges would oversee the forfeiture of assets, applying the necessary protections of due process, ensuring that only "tainted" property is seized, and ensuring that the requisite connection with criminal gang activity is established. For two decades, the courts of the United States have reviewed the civil forfeiture provisions of U.S. law dealing with drug trafficking, and have repeatedly held these provisions to be constitutional, while delineating the specific procedural protections that must be provided. The proposed amendments that I have submitted to this committee will likewise withstand constitutional scrutiny.

Civil forfeiture of assets has substantially altered the playing field in favor of law enforcement in the war against drugs. Through the use of civil forfeiture, prosecutors are not only able to incarcerate drug dealers, but also able to hobble their operations financially. We must similarly change the game in immigration enforcement if we are to stop criminal gang members from entering and reentering the United States with impunity. Such aliens not only have no right to prey upon our society, they have no right to the proceeds of their violent and destructive activity.

4

Deportation Laws Will Not Decrease Gang Violence

Sheila Jackson Lee and David Cole

Sheila Jackson Lee is a Democratic member of the U.S. House of Representatives from Houston, Texas. David Cole is a professor at Georgetown University Law Center in Washington, D.C.

The United States does not need nor should it approve new legislation for the deportation of alien gang members. The proposed legislation, the Alien Gang Removal Act (AGRA), would give the U.S. attorney general the power to deport foreign nationals—including legal permanent residents—solely because of their alleged gang affiliation, even if they have never committed a crime. While gang violence is a problem in the United States, it can be dealt with through existing laws that focus on those gang members who have committed serious crimes. Current law dictates that any foreign national gang member who breaks the law can be deported. The proposed law reaches too far over the ethical line of a free society and of the First Amendment itself by holding people responsible for the actions of others with whom they have been associated.

The Justice Department [in June 2005] issued a little-noticed report finding that, contrary to popular perception, gang violence has dropped dramatically over the past decade. The percentage of violent crimes committed by gang members fell by 73 percent from 1994 to 2003.

Sheila Jackson Lee and David Cole, "Wrong Weapon to Fight Alien Gangs; Proposed Legislation Outdated, Ineffective," HoustonChronicle.com, July 23, 2005. Reproduced by permission of the authors.

Yet, members of Congress are acting as if gang crime is exploding, and proposing laws that would repeat some of the worst sins of the past, from guilt by association to the resurrection of an attorney general's list of blacklisted groups.

The New Laws Are Unjust

The House has already passed one gang bill that, among other things, would make nonviolent misdemeanors grounds for deportation. And now Republicans have introduced the Alien Gang Removal Act (AGRA), which goes even further. It would give the attorney general virtually unfettered power to designate any of thousands of gangs in the United States, and would then make automatically deportable any foreign national deemed to be a member of such a gang.

The Law would apply even to legal permanent residents who had never committed a crime. It would apply to young children, often the target of gang recruiting drives. And it would require us to return an individual to a country where he faced persecution, based solely on his perceived associations.

We agree that gang crime remains a problem, although the Justice Department's own statistics show that much of the rhetoric about the problem is hyperbole not grounded in fact. But we think the problem can be dealt with through existing laws, by focusing on gang members who commit serious crimes, rather than extending such harsh consequences to individuals who have never committed a crime in their lives.

Other Methods Are More Effective

Our country has generally relied on three strategies for dealing with youth gangs: suppression, which has meant longer criminal sentences and penalties; intervention, through job training, education and skills development in an attempt to reform gang members; and prevention, through school- and community-based programs designed to reach out to at-risk children before they become involved with gangs.

For instance, the Rev. Gregory Boyle, a Jesuit priest in Los Angeles known as G-Dog or Father Greg, began Homeboy Industries in 1992, a job-training program to salvage the futures of gang members. Many of his employees had long arrest and prison records, and nearly all had no work skills. But Boyle and Homeboy Industries officials have counseled and found jobs for several thousand youths from 500 Los Angeles gangs.

What AGRA would do is make immigrants deportable who had never violated the law.

Immigration law can also be an appropriate tool for targeting gang crime. Under current law, any foreign national gang member who violates the terms of his visa can be deported, as can any foreign national gang member who has committed a deportable criminal offense. Thus, where an immigrant gang member has broken the law, he is generally deportable under current law.

New Deportation Law Would Violate Civil Rights

What AGRA would do is make immigrants deportable who had never violated the law, based solely on their alleged membership in a designated gang. That is guilt by association; it holds people responsible not for their own actions, but for the actions of others with whom they have associated.

We have seen this kind of approach before.

In the 1950s, at the height of the Cold War, Congress made it a deportable offense and a crime merely to be a member of the Communist Party. At the same time, the attorney general created a subversive organizations list as the basis for imposing guilt by association even further.

The McCarthy era taught us a lesson: namely, that guilt by association, as the Supreme Court has said, is alien to the traditions of a free society and the First Amendment itself.

But apparently some have forgotten that lesson. Under this bill, the attorney general would again have a subversive organizations list. The gangs listed would have no right to challenge their designation by offering evidence that the designation was wrong. And individuals charged as members of the gang would be expressly barred from challenging the designation. It would be no defense to show that one had never committed any crime, or that one's gang had never committed a crime.

The politics behind such efforts also echo the McCarthy era. Sen. Joe McCarthy was driven as much by a partisan desire to paint his Democratic opponents as soft on communism as by any actual threat communists posed. So, too, today, nothing could be easier, as a political matter, than to go after alien gang members. But in responding to the problem of gang crime, we should be driven by facts and principles, not pure politics.

Federal Gang Task Forces Will Thwart Gang Violence

Chris Swecker

Chris Swecker is assistant director of the Criminal Investigative Division at the Federal Bureau of Investigation.

Gang violence has become one of the greatest threats to the safety of all Americans. There are an estimated eight hundred thousand gang members across the United States involved in drug dealing, weapons trafficking, rape, murder, extortion, alien smuggling, auto theft, and robbery. In order to combat and dismantle these dangerous gangs—especially the violent Mara Salvatrucha (MS-13) gang—the FBI has established national gang task forces to enable local, state, federal, and international law enforcement agencies to identify gang members and shut down their criminal activities. The FBI expects the task forces to be successful in protecting America's citizens against gang violence.

Gangs and other criminal enterprises, operating in the U.S. and throughout the world, pose increasing concerns for the international law enforcement and intelligence communities. Today, gangs are more violent, more organized, and more widespread than ever before. They pose one of the greatest threats to the safety and security of all Americans. The Department of Justice estimates there are approximately 30,000 gangs, with 800,000 members, impacting 2,500 communities across the U.S. The innocent people in these communities face daily exposure to violence from criminal gangs trafficking in

Chris Swecker, statement before the Subcommittee on the Western Hemisphere House International Relations Committee, April 20, 2005.

drugs and weapons and gangs fighting amongst themselves to control or extend their turf and their various criminal enterprises.

The Rapid Proliferation of Gangs

Gangs from California, particularly in the Los Angeles area, have a major influence on Mexican-American and Central American gangs in this country and in Latin America. Hispanic gangs in California have separated into two rival factions, the Nortenos, which are primarily found in Northern California, and the Surenos, found to the south and predominantly in the urban areas surrounding Los Angeles. A rivalry exists between these factions, which had its genesis in the California Department of Corrections during the 1960s, when the Nuestra Familia (Nortenos) prison gang formed to oppose the Mexican Mafia (Surenos) prison gang. Today, the Mexican Mafia, and other Hispanic prison gangs, such as the La EME in southern California, the Texas Syndicate (T/S, Syndicato Tejano), and the Mexikanemi (EMI, Texas Mexican Mafia) remain powerful both in prison and on the street, and most Hispanic gangs in California align themselves under the Nortenos or the Surenos. Hispanic gangs aligned under the Nortenos will generally add the number 14 after their gang name, while gangs aligned under the Surenos will generally add the number 13 (i.e., MS-13).

The migration of MS-13 members and other Hispanic street gang members, such as 18th Street, from Southern California to other regions of this country has led to a rapid proliferation of these gangs in many smaller, suburban, and rural areas not accustomed to gang activity and related crimes. Additionally, the deportation of MS-13 and 18th Street gang members from the United States to their countries of origin is partially responsible for the growth of those gangs in El Salvador, Honduras, Guatemala, and Mexico, although the precise [level] of this responsibility is unknown.

Major urban areas such as Chicago and New York have also experienced major gang activity associated with Latino gangs for decades. In Chicago, the Almighty Latin King Nation (ALKN) was founded in the 1940s by a small group of Hispanics, many of Puerto Rican descent. At first, the organization aspired to meet the personal, social, and economic needs of the members and the preservation of cultural heritage. Today, the Latin Kings in Chicago have chapters consisting primarily of members of Mexican descent and chapters consisting of membership of Puerto Rican descent. Numerous chapters now exist in multiple states and are involved in an array of criminal activity.

In response to the growing threat from gangs, the FBI has raised the priority of gang intelligence and investigative efforts.

A National Antigang Strategy

To address the threat these and other gangs pose on a local, regional, national, and even international level, the FBI established a National Gang Strategy to identify the gangs posing the greatest danger to American communities, to combine and coordinate the efforts of local, state, and federal law enforcement in Safe Streets Violent Gang Task Forces throughout the U.S., and to utilize the same statutes and intelligence and investigative techniques, previously used against organized crime, against violent gangs. . . .

In response to the growing threat from gangs, the FBI has raised the priority of gang intelligence and investigative efforts by increasing the number of Safe Streets Violent Gang Task Forces (SSVGTF) from 78 to 108, with the ultimate goal of increasing this number to 128. From FY [fiscal year] 1996 to 2004, the SSVGTF realized the following accomplishments:

- Arrests: 41,747

- Information/Indictments: 19,560

- Convictions: 19,166

- Disruptions: 846

- Dismantlements: 253

- Title IIIs: 1,460

- Undercover Operations: 109

- RICO Informations/Indictments: 533

Additionally, the FBI is in the process of establishing a National Gang Intelligence Center (NGIC) and has established the MS-13 National Gang Task Force (NGTF).

MS-13 members and associates now have a presence in more than 31 states and the District of Columbia.

The NGIC will enable the FBI and its local, state, and federal partners to centralize and coordinate the national collection of intelligence on gangs in the U.S., and then analyze, share, and disseminate this intelligence with law enforcement authorities throughout the country. The NGIC will give local, state and federal investigators and intelligence analysts the opportunity and mechanism to share their collective information and intelligence on gangs. This will enable gang investigators and analysts to identify links between gangs and gang investigations, to further identify gangs and gang members, to learn the full scope of their criminal activities and enterprises, to determine which gangs pose the greatest threat to the U.S., to identify trends in gang activity and migration, and to guide them in coordinating their investigations and prosecutions to disrupt and dismantle gangs. The NGIC will be an essential part of our efforts to combat and dismantle gangs and will enhance the existing liaison and coordination efforts of federal, state, and local agencies. . . .

The Threat of MS-13

One of the gangs being addressed by the FBI and its law enforcement partners under the National Gang Strategy is the Mara Salvatrucha (MS-13). MS-13 is a violent gang comprised primarily of Central American immigrants which originated in Los Angeles and has now spread across the country. MS-13 gang members are primarily from El Salvador, Honduras, and Guatemala, who initially established a presence in Los Angeles, California, in the 1980s. In 1993, three MS-13 gang members from Los Angeles, California, moved to the Northern Virginia and Washington, DC, metropolitan area to recruit additional MS-13 members. Current reporting now estimates there are as many as 1500 members of MS-13 in the Northern Virginia/DC area.

Based upon the National Gang Threat Assessment conducted by the National Alliance of Gang Investigators Association, MS-13 members and associates now have a presence in more than 31 states and the District of Columbia. MS-13 has a significant presence in Northern Virginia, New York, California, Texas, as well as in places as disparate and widespread as Oregon City, Oregon, and Omaha, Nebraska. Due to the lack of a national database and standard reporting criteria for the identification of gang members, the frequent use of aliases by gang members, and the transient nature of gang members, the actual number of MS-13 members in the United States is difficult to determine. However, the National Drug Intelligence Center estimates there to be between 8,000 and 10,000 hardcore members in MS-13. . . .

Law enforcement in 28 states have reported MS-13 members are engaged in retail drug trafficking, primarily trafficking in powdered cocaine, crack cocaine, and marijuana, and, to a lesser extent, in methamphetamine and heroin. The drug proceeds are then laundered through seemingly legitimate businesses in those communities. MS-13 members are also involved in a variety of other types of criminal activity, including rape, murder, extortion, auto theft, alien smuggling, and robbery.

Given the extreme violence exhibited by MS-13 and its potential threat, based on the historical precedent of other similar gangs and organized criminal organizations, the FBI established the MS-13 National Gang Task Force to disrupt and dismantle this gang, now, before it has the opportunity to become more organized and sophisticated and more difficult to attack. The goals of the MS-13 National Gang Task Force are to enable local, state, and federal, as well as international law enforcement agencies, to easily exchange information on MS-13; to enable local and state law enforcement agencies to identify the presence of MS-13 in their territories; to identify related investigations; and to coordinate regional and/or nationwide, multi-jurisdictional law enforcement action, including federal Racketeering (RICO) and Violent Crimes in Aid of Racketeering (VICAR) prosecutions. . . .

International Cooperation

Extensive contact has also been made with the law enforcement community in Honduras, Guatemala, and El Salvador, by both the MS-13 task force leadership and our Office of International Operations, in order to share intelligence and begin a coordinated effort to address MS-13 street gangs both nationally and internationally. The FBI and other federal agencies recently attended the first International Gang Conference held in San Salvador, El Salvador, where the FBI succeeded in gaining the support of El Salvador's cooperation and participation in joint, international efforts against MS-13. At present, the FBI has one Legal Attaché in Panama that provides coverage to this region. Efforts are currently underway to establish a resident FBI presence in El Salvador.

As an example of the MS-13 National Gang Task Force coordination efforts, in early February 2005, the FBI, Customs and Border Patrol, Texas Department of Public Safety, and the East Hidalgo Detention Center worked together to arrest a key MS-13 figure. This individual is alleged to have been involved in a bus massacre that took place in Honduras on December 23, 2004, wherein a total of 28 people were assassinated, including 6 children. Fourteen other individuals were seriously wounded. A note left at the scene indicated the massacre was in retaliation against laws targeting gang members in Honduras, and MS-13 members were identified as being responsible for the attack. . . .

The FBI will continue its efforts, and we will keep this Committee [on International Relations] informed of our progress in protecting this nation's citizens against gangs and other criminal enterprises, particularly those with national and international implications.

6

Federal Gang Task Forces Will Not Thwart Gang Violence

Luis J. Rodriguez

Luis J. Rodriguez is a published author and has worked interna-tionally with troubled youth for thirty years.

To prevent gang violence, the FBI created task forces to hunt down and lock up gang members; however, to fund those task forces, approximately 4 billion dollars was cut from the much needed and highly successful crime prevention programs that have provided treatment, jobs, and education for young people. Experts who work with gang members understand that gang warfare cannot be stopped with more warfare. The solution to gang violence is well-funded and long-range prevention pro-grams that help children in the poorest neighborhoods—not fed-eral gang task forces.

When First Lady Laura Bush visited Homeboy Industries in the Los Angeles barrio of Boyle Heights on April 27 [2005], eyebrows went up among some people who have worked with hardened gang youth: What was a Republican, former librarian, and President Bush's much better half doing among tattooed, brown-skinned men who had been shot, had done some shootings, and were often portrayed in the media as "the worst of the worst"?

Laura Bush was ostensibly on a mission, fueled by $150 million, called "Helping America's Youth," which President Bush had announced in his February 6 [2005] State of the Union address.

Gang Members Need to Be Heard

Mrs. Bush listened as Homeboy Industries founder Father Gregory Boyle showed her around while former gang members greeted her. She had one question for thirty-one-year-old Alex Zamudio, a baker in Homeboy's Bakery, who lost an eye at age thirteen after being shot: "When you were a child and you went and chose the path to go to a gang, do you think there was anything you could have done at that point in your life that would have directed you another way?"

"Everywhere we grew up was gang infested," Alex answered. "You grow up into that—either family members or people you go to school with. Everybody you are involved with is in gangs, so you end up being a gang member."

I know Alex. He's a formidable, large-framed man with close-cropped hair. He has seen the barrio gang life from the inside out. For him, joining a gang wasn't a choice. He lived in neighborhoods where gangs have been around for several generations—grandfather to father to son—where gangs proved to be the best organized means to get attention, respect, and even money.

In late May, Alex played a mentoring role for around fifty teens from Watts, South Central, Boyle Heights/East L.A., the San Fernando Valley, Seattle, San Francisco, and Chicago during a "Voices of Youth, Voices of Community" youth conference I helped facilitate in the Malibu Hills. Despite many difficulties, including having youngsters who didn't know how to write, Alex worked hard to get most of these young men and women to write their lives. They came up with some harrowing stories that they later read to an audience of 200 people at

Mount Saint Mary's College, near downtown L.A. Alex also read a piece about his former existence he called "My Wicked Past."

The Focus Should Be on Prevention

I give Laura Bush credit—for giving gang youth credence and respect. But at the very time the First Lady was visiting Homeboy Industries, the White House was pushing the "Gangbusters" bill. Two weeks later, the Republican-dominated House of Representatives had approved it. Among other things, it turns gang-related violent offenses into federal crimes punishable by mandatory sentences from ten years to life, adds the death penalty to sentencing guidelines, and authorizes the prosecution of youth from age sixteen as adults in federal courts.

Already the Congressional Budget Office estimates the bill's cost to reach $62 million in the first four years, primarily with the increased growth of the federal prison population—from 100 prisoners the first year to around 900 a year by 2010. I think it will be far worse.

In the same budget package that funded "Helping America's Youth," President Bush proposed cutting $4.2 billion from youth and crime-prevention programs: That's twenty-eight times what he offered the First Lady. The cuts include $34.7 million from the Elementary and Secondary School Counseling Program and close to a 20 percent reduction for the Boys & Girls Clubs of America, one of the groups Laura Bush has touted as a viable "community-based center" for youth.

While Mrs. Bush may be genuine in her efforts, her husband's anti-gang policies have a clear and linked purpose. The overall objective is to shrink the federal government's role in society to primarily military operations and complicated domestic security measures (including against street gangs, now labeled "domestic terrorists"). Billions of dollars have already poured into Afghanistan, Iraq, and other international hot spots; billions are also pouring into Homeland Security and local law enforcement.

Socially relevant programs, on the other hand, that provide treatment, jobs, education, arts, and after-school recreation will fall more and more into private hands. . . .

Anyone seriously working these streets knows you can't stop gang warfare with more warfare.

The Federal Government Declares War Against Gangs

The White House and Congress are waging all-out war against street gangs (although anyone seriously working these streets knows you can't stop gang warfare with more warfare). [In May 2005], the FBI outlined its anti-gang strategy on the agency's website, courtesy of their top criminal investigative executive, Chris Swecker.

"Gangs and other criminal enterprises, operating in the U.S. and throughout the world, pose increasing concerns for the international law enforcement and intelligence communities," Swecker declared. "Today gangs are more violent, more organized, and more widespread than ever before. They pose one of the greatest threats to the safety and security of all Americans. The Department of Justice estimates there are approximately 30,000 gangs, with 800,000 members, impacting 2,500 communities in the U.S."

In the FBI's crosshairs is the Mara Salvatrucha, or MS-13, a street gang that began in Los Angeles in the mid-1980s and then spread throughout the United States and Canada, but most notably to El Salvador, Guatemala, Honduras, and Mexico.

"Gangs from California, particularly in the Los Angeles area, have a major influence on Mexican American and Central American gangs in this country and in Latin America," added Swecker.

Also on the FBI's list of the most dangerous street gangs are Nortenos (Northern California Latino gangs allied to the Nuestra Familia prison organization), Surenos (Southern California gangs allied to the Mexican Mafia prison organization), Latin Kings (mostly in Chicago, New York City, and other Midwest and East Coast communities), and street organizations in Texas, Arizona, and Puerto Rico.

Part of the FBI's strategy, Swecker pointed out, is to create a National Gang Intelligence Center and to establish the MS-13 National Gang Task Force.

It will take caring, active, trusting, and respectful adults in the lives of all our youth [to bring peace to the streets].

Force Will Not Prevent Gang Violence

But I fear these policies will adversely affect people like Alex Zamudio. Many of the youth I've worked with have now left the gang life. They have families, jobs, and careers. Still they can become police targets just for having been a gang member, living around gang members, or having tattoos.

I fear for Jose, one of the gang youth who took part in the "Voices of Youth." After he returned from Malibu, he got jumped. But he decided to choose life over death by refusing to take part in retaliation. (His mentors have been watching over him, since this act in itself can endanger his life.)

And I fear for the many MS members who've become active in Homies Unidos, a peace and justice organization made up of former gang youth in Central America and L.A., but who have also been harassed by police and immigration authorities nationwide.

If more jail terms and police presence doesn't work, what does?

Fortunately, this is no mystery.

Talk to Father Greg Boyle.

Talk to Silvia Beltran of Homies Unidos.

Talk to Freddy Calixto of Chicago's BUILD.

Talk to Aqeela Sherrills, a leader in the Crips-Bloods truce of Watts.

There are hundreds more like them in the poorest, most neglected neighborhoods, working diligently with scarce resources—and for far longer than Laura Bush—in bringing peace to our streets.

It will take caring, active, trusting, and respectful adults in the lives of all our youth—although most adults are overworked, tired, and often just plain poor.

It will take creative engagement through words, art, song, dance, story, and paint—although most arts and creative programs are the first to be cut during a financial crisis.

It will take jobs that won't demean or degrade a person's spirit—although jobs are leaving this country at monumental rates, particularly for young people.

It will take schools that are small enough for the adults to care for each child, yet resourceful enough to provide the skills, creativity, and knowledge to help students become competent and confident in any field of life they choose to do—although schools are being shortchanged by most states and Bush's "No Child Left Behind" is leaving children in the poorest neighborhoods far behind.

The fact is we don't need mixed messages. We don't need the "carrot and the stick" (which in this case is mostly stick and not much carrot). We don't need suppression, sprinkled with prevention.

An all-out effort—as much as it took to topple two governments and send many of our young people to their deaths [in the wars in Iraq and Afghanistan]—would help.

Real well-funded and long-range prevention—and real genuine and healthy intervention would help.

More funds into already proven programs like Head Start would help, but I'm also talking about sustained attention and resources into imaginative, holistic, natural, and community-derived urban peace plans embracing all members of the community, including gang members themselves. Peace without the gangs won't last. Incorporate them in the peace we all need; don't push them out. And, yes, include the schools, churches, businesses, families, law enforcement, community centers, treatment centers, and more—as part of a whole package, not just piecemeal, band-aid responses.

A month after Laura Bush's visit to Homeboy's Bakery, I caught up with Alex Zamudio.

"We need more 'Voices of Youth,' where I can talk to kids about my past experiences and we can listen to them about what they're going through," he told me. "It's about reaching out to the youngsters. I've lived that life, involved in crime, a life that leads to death or jail. I let this life go. Now I want to talk to them so they won't have to go through this."

I vote for that.

7

Closing the Borders Will Reduce Gang Violence

Heather Mac Donald

Heather Mac Donald is a published author and senior fellow at the Manhattan Institute for Policy Research, a think tank in New York City.

Though most are hardworking and law abiding, immigrants from Latin America and Mexico are creating an underclass in the United States. Hispanic youth drop out of school in greater numbers than any other group and are contributing to an explosion of gang activity. In many cities Hispanic youth as young as nine years old are recruited into gangs and become involved in such violent crimes as home invasion, robbery, battery, drug sales, and rape. The United States needs to close its borders and enforce its immigration laws to prevent the skyrocketing gang crime and violence caused by the constant influx of illegal immigrants arriving from Mexico and Latin America.

Before immigration optimists issue another rosy prognosis for America's multicultural future, they might visit Belmont High School in Los Angeles's overwhelmingly Hispanic, gang-ridden Rampart district. "Upward and onward" is not a phrase that comes to mind when speaking to the first- and second-generation immigrant teens milling around the school. . . .

"Most of the people I used to hang out with when I first came to the school have dropped out," observes Jackie, a viva-

Heather Mac Donald, "The Immigrant Gang Plague," *City Journal*, Summer 2004.
Copyright The Manhattan Institute. Reproduced by permission.

cious illegal alien from Guatemala. "Others got kicked out or got into drugs. Five graduated, and four home girls got pregnant." . . .

Hispanic Youth Are Creating an Underclass Culture

These Belmont teens are no aberration. Hispanic youths, whether recent arrivals or birthright American citizens, are developing an underclass culture. (By "Hispanic" here, I mean the population originating in Latin America—above all, in Mexico—as distinct from America's much smaller Puerto Rican and Dominican communities of Caribbean descent, which have themselves long shown elevated crime and welfare rates.) Hispanic school dropout rates and teen birthrates are now the highest in the nation. Gang crime is exploding nationally—rising 50 percent from 1999 to 2002—driven by the march of Hispanic immigration east and north across the country. Most worrisome, underclass indicators like crime and single parenthood do not improve over successive generations of Hispanics—they worsen.

Debate has recently heated up over whether Mexican immigration—unique in its scale and in other important ways—will defeat the American tradition of assimilation. The rise of underclass behavior among the progeny of Mexicans and other Central Americans must be part of that debate. There may be assimilation going on, but a significant portion of it is assimilation downward to the worst elements of American life. To be sure, most Hispanics are hardworking, law-abiding residents; they have reclaimed squalid neighborhoods in South Central Los Angeles and elsewhere. Among the dozens of Hispanic youths I interviewed, several expressed gratitude for the United States, a sentiment that would be hard to find among the ordinary run of teenagers. But given the magnitude of present immigration levels, if only a portion of those from south of the border goes bad, the costs to society will be enormous. . . .

David O'Connell, pastor of the church next door to Soledad [Enrichment Action Charter School in South Central Los Angeles] has been fighting L.A.'s gang culture for over a decade. He rues the "ferocious stuff" that is currently coming out of Central America, sounding weary and pessimistic. But "what's more frightening," he says, "is the disengagement from adults." Hispanic children feel that they have to deal with problems themselves, apart from their parents, according to O'Connell, and they "do so in violent ways." The adults, for their part, start to fear young people, including their own children.

Recruitment is starting early in middle school.

Gangs Recruit Hispanic Children

The pull to a culture of violence among Hispanic children begins earlier and earlier, O'Connell says. Researchers and youth workers across the country confirm his observation. In Chicago, gangs start recruiting kids at age nine, according to criminologists studying policing and social trends in the Windy City. The Chicago Community Policing Evaluation Consortium concluded that gangs have become fully integrated into Hispanic youth culture; even children not in gangs emulate their attitudes, dress, and self-presentation. The result is a community in thrall. Non-affiliated children fear traveling into unknown neighborhoods and sometimes drop out of school for lack of protection. Adults are just as scared. They may know who has been spray-painting their garage, for example, but won't tell the police for fear that their car will be torched in retaliation. "It's like we're in our own little jails that we can't leave," said a resident. "There isn't an uninfested place nearby."

Washington, D.C., reports the same "ever-younger" phenomenon. "Recruitment is starting early in middle school," says Lori Kaplan, head of D.C.'s Latin American Youth Center.

51

With early recruitment comes a high school dropout rate of 50 percent. "Gang culture is gaining more recruits than our ability to get kids out," Kaplan laments. "We can get this kid out, but two or three will take his place." In May, an 18-year-old member of the Salvadoran Mara Salvatrucha gang used a machete to chop off four left fingers and nearly sever the right hand of a 16-year-old South Side Locos rival in the Washington suburbs. . . .

This is beyond a regional problem. It is, in fact, a national problem.

Hispanic Gangs Are Growing Increasingly Violent

The constant invasion of illegal aliens is worsening gang violence as well. In Phoenix, Arizona, and surrounding Maricopa County, illegal alien gangs, such as Brown Pride and Wetback Power, are growing more volatile and dangerous, according to Tom Bearup, a former sheriff's department official and current candidate for sheriff. Even in prison, where they clash with American Hispanics, they are creating a more vicious environment.

Upward mobility to the suburbs doesn't necessarily break the allure of gang culture. An immigration agent reports that in the middle-class suburbs of southwest Miami, second- and third-generation Hispanic youths are perpetrating home invasions, robberies, battery, drug sales, and rape. [Santa Ana, California, police officer and gang investigator] Kevin Ruiz knows students at the University of California, Irvine, who retain their gang connections. Prosecutors in formerly crime-free Ventura County, California, sought an injunction [in May 2004] against the Colonia Chiques gang after homicides rocketed up; an affidavit supporting the injunction details how Chiques members terrorize the local hospital whenever one of the gang arrives with a gunshot wound. Federal law enforcement officials in Virginia are tracking with alarm the spread of gang violence from Northern Virginia west into the Shenandoah Valley and south toward Charlottesville, a trend so disturbing that they secured federal funds to stanch the mayhem. "This is beyond a regional problem. It is, in fact, a national problem," said FBI assistant director Michael Mason, head of the bureau's Washington field office.

Open-borders apologists dismiss the Hispanic crime threat by observing that black crime rates are even higher. True, but irrelevant: the black population is not growing, whereas Hispanic immigration is reaching virtually every part of the country, sometimes radically changing local demographics. With a felony arrest rate up to triple that of whites, Hispanics can dramatically raise community crime levels.

Hispanic Culture Perpetuates the Gang Problem

Many cops and youth workers blame the increase in gang appeal on the disintegration of the Hispanic family. The trends are worsening, especially for U.S.-born Hispanics. In California, 67 percent of children of U.S.-born Hispanic parents lived in an intact family in 1990; by 1999, that number had dropped to 56 percent. The percentage of Hispanic children living with a single mother in California rose from 18 percent in 1990 to 29 percent in 1999. Nationally, single-parent households constituted 25 percent of all Hispanic households with minor children in 1980; by 2000, the proportion had jumped to 34 percent. . . .

In one respect, Central American immigrants break the mold of traditional American underclass behavior: they work. Even so, Mexican welfare receipt is twice as high as that of natives, in large part because Mexican-American incomes are so low, and remain low over successive generations. Disturbingly, welfare use actually rises between the second and third generation—to 31 percent of all third-generation Mexican-

American households. Illegal Hispanics make liberal use of welfare, too, by putting their American-born children on public assistance: in Orange County, California, nearly twice as many Hispanic welfare cases are for children of illegal aliens as for legal families.

More troublingly, some Hispanics combine work with gangbanging. Gang detectives in Long Island's Suffolk County know when members of the violent Salvadoran MS-13 gang get off work from their lawn-maintenance or pizzeria jobs, and can follow them to their gang meetings. Mexican gang members in rural Pennsylvania, which saw two gang homicides in late April [2004] also often work in landscaping and construction.

The Dropout Rate in Schools Is High

On the final component of underclass behavior—school failure—Hispanics are in a class by themselves. No other group drops out in greater numbers. In Los Angeles, only 48 percent of Hispanic ninth-graders graduate, compared with a 56 percent citywide graduation rate and a 70 percent nationwide rate. In 2000, nearly 30 percent of Hispanics between the ages of 16 and 24 were high school dropouts nationwide, compared with about 13 percent of blacks and about 7 percent of whites.

The constant inflow of barely literate recent Mexican arrivals unquestionably brings down Hispanic education levels. But later, American-born generations don't brighten the picture much. While Mexican-Americans make significant education gains between the first and second generation, adding 3.5 years of schooling, progress stalls in the next generation, economists Jeffrey Grogger and Stephen Trejo have found. Third-generation Mexican-Americans remain three times as likely to drop out of high school than whites and one and a half times as likely to drop out as blacks. They complete college at one-third the rate of whites. Mexican-Americans are assimilating not to the national schooling average, observed the Federal Reserve Bank of Dallas this June [2004], but to the dramatically lower "Hispanic average." In educational outcomes, concluded the bank, "Ethnicity matters."

No one knows why this is so. Every parent I spoke to said that she wanted her children to do well in school and go to college. Yet the message is often not getting across. "Hispanic parents are the kind of parents that leave it to others," explains an unwed Salvadoran welfare mother in Santa Ana. "We don't get that involved." A news director of a Southern California Spanish radio station expresses frustration at the passivity toward education and upward mobility he sees in his own family. "I tried to knock the 'Spanglish' accent out of my niece and get rid of that crap," he says. "But the mother was completely nihilistic about her child. It's going to take direct action from Americans to Americanize Hispanics." . . .

Maintaining the current open-borders regime is folly.

Hispanic Immigrants Differ from Other Immigrants

Without prompting, Ruiz brings up the million-dollar question: "I don't see assimilation," he says. "They want to hold on [to Hispanic culture]." Ruiz thinks that today's Mexican immigrant is a "totally different kind of person" from the past. Some come with a chip on their shoulder toward the United States, he says, which they blame for the political and economic failure of their home countries. Rather than aggressively seizing the opportunities available to them, especially in education, they have learned to play the victim card, he thinks. Ruiz advocates a much more aggressive approach. "We need to explain, 'We'll help you assimilate up to a certain point, but then you have to take advantage of what's here.'"

Ruiz's observations will strike anyone who has hired eager Mexican and Central American workers as incredible. I pressed him repeatedly, insisting that Americans see Mexican immigrants as cheerful and hardworking, but he was adamant. "We're creating an underclass," he maintained.

Immigration optimists, ever ready to trumpet the benefits of today's immigration wave, have refused to acknowledge its costs. Foremost among them are skyrocketing gang crime and an expanding underclass. Until the country figures out how to reduce these costs, maintaining the current open borders regime is folly. We should enforce our immigration laws and select immigrants on skills and likely upward mobility, not success in sneaking across the border.

8

Closing the Borders Will Not Reduce Gang Violence

Jim Rogers

Jim Rogers is a published author who also writes a monthly column for his Web site, www.jimrogers.com.

Most immigrants come to the United States in hopes of finding a better life; however, many Americans oppose their arrival, fearing that immigrants will form gangs and pose a danger to American society. These Americans argue that the borders should be closed to immigrants; however, closing the borders will not protect Americans from violence. On the contrary, opening the borders to people who are brave and ambitious enough to try to enter the United States will only help America prosper because such ambitious people are just what the country needs. To prevent violence, including violence committed by gangs, the United States should instead focus on improving its domestic policies.

It seems like every time I open a newspaper or watch the news these days there's another story about a boatload of Haitians caught trying to make their way into the U.S. or the tale of a rail car full of Mexicans dying as they cross the border. Getting into our country, after all, is the dream of so many who want to start anew, or at least have a chance at a better life. The immigration issue is a topic of great debate among politicians and lobbyists, media pundits and scholars, conservatives and liberals alike, a controversy that strikes at the heart of this country's identity as a melting pot. It's also a

Jim Rogers, "Open the Doors," www.jimrogers.com, December 3, 2002. Reproduced by permission.

particularly sticky issue these days, as visions of foreign terrorists continue to loom in our minds.

Americans Should Welcome Differences

Those opposing immigration everywhere throughout history always use the same reasons, especially "These immigrants are different from the ones before."

Remember how Americans complained bitterly that the Irish were "different" from previous immigrants when they came here in the mid-19th century? They were "drunks and outlaws and formed gangs". And, horror of horrors, they were a different religion; they were Roman Catholic. Then later we really got a wave of "different immigrants". We got Italians and southern Europeans who spoke different languages and ate smelly food and were "Papists"; "They could never be loyal Americans because they would obey Rome." "And they form gangs."

The anti-immigrant idea that they were different was so strong and lasted so long that it was inconceivable that a Catholic could be elected President for 170 years. Jack Kennedy changed that, of course, but was America destroyed from within or from without because we had Catholics invade our shores?

Later generations said the same about the Jews, the Chinese, the Eastern Europeans, the Poles, the Germans, the Ethiopians, the Cubans, the Dominicans, the Vietnamese, everyone at one time or another. "This group of immigrants is different from before" which really means they are a different religion or ethnic group or linguistic group. "Their food smells bad and so do they"—even though they work harder than anyone else just as all immigrants have had to do throughout history everywhere. For decades Asians could not even own property in the US because they were "different".

All of these arguments sound ludicrous now just as will the current set of "differences" seem absurd in a few years. In

Schenectady [New York] the Mayor is out recruiting Guyanese immigrants now because they add so much to his city. I remember seeing on TV once a Cuban who had strapped himself to a barrel to get to America. The police arrested him as he washed ashore. I would have been there hiring him instead the moment he washed ashore.

Closing our doors to outsiders isn't going to make the U.S. any safer.

Do we really think America would have been better off if we had kept out the Irish, Italians, Asians, Jews, Poles, Germans, Ethiopians, Dominicans, etc., etc. Should we send them all back? Every one of these groups and others were considered different at one time or another and many argued to close the doors because of them.

Immigrants Contribute to America

Here's my solution: Let 'em all in. Get rid of visas and passports. Do away with custom agents and the Immigration and Naturalization Service [INS]. Those people who are ambitious and brave enough to risk it all to get here are exactly the kind of people we want in this country. They are certainly the kind of people I would want working for me. That kind of enterprising attitude is exactly what made this country great. Plus, closing our doors to outsiders isn't going to make the U.S. any safer. No country in history has lost a war because of visas. . . .

Today, there are about 33.1 million immigrants (both legal and illegal) living in the U.S. That means that roughly one in every eight people is foreign-born. Mexico, naturally, is the largest source of our immigrant population, with just under 10 million Mexicans living in the U.S., according to a recent study by the Center for Immigration Studies. Another 50,000 immigrants enter the U.S. annually through the State

Department's Green Card lottery system, which admits people from countries with low-rates of immigration to the U.S.

Such a foreign presence within our borders may sound disturbing to some but the reality is that we need these people just as our forebears were needed. Don't think that these are just uneducated laborers, looking to steal American jobs. However, even the laborers are needed since Americans will not take many of the jobs, preferring unemployment or welfare instead. Many immigrants are highly skilled workers who bring their talents (and their capital) where they can best be used. Of the legal immigrants living here in the U.S., 21 percent have at least 17 years of education, which often includes graduate or professional schools. Among Americans born here, only 8 percent can boast such expertise. . . .

We are much more likely to be murdered or harmed by family members or friends than by foreigners.

Fear Is No Excuse to Close Borders

Those who opposed a more liberal immigration policy ultimately point to security as the biggest reason we should tighten our borders. After all, the man who shot and killed two people at the Los Angeles airport [on] July 4 [2002] was admitted through the Green Card Lottery. John Lee Malvo, the Washington D.C. sniper, was an illegal immigrant who somehow evaded the INS. Like everyone else, I certainly want to live in a safe environment, but remember "security" is a common ruse used by isolationists to promote various causes. Protectionists limit foreign mohair coming into the U.S. in the name of national defense. Even foreign sugar is limited in the name of security.

There is even a movement to deport immigrants because they are "dangerous," but we are much more likely to be murdered or harmed by family members or friends than by foreigners in the U.S. Shall we deport our mothers and children too?

That said, fear should not be used as an excuse for what's best for our country and what's best for our society and economy. Let's not forget the events of Oklahoma City, which reminded us that terrorism is a domestic problem as much as an international one. The McVeigh family had been here for generations as had the family of John Allen Williams, the mastermind of the D.C. snipers. The Unibomber was a former professor and Harvard graduate. The solution is not to close our borders. Instead, we need to have better policies and programs to insure freedoms and prosperity here. Immigrants, legal or illegal are here to stay. That's not likely to change. I'm no expert, but I would imagine that we'd have better luck rooting out the bad seeds if we embraced those who want to come to our country, rather than having so many people try to slip in surreptitiously.

Short-sighted measures now will only hurt us in the end. Ben Franklin lived here in a period of wars and revolution. A third of the population opposed the Revolution and were "subversives." The colonies were surrounded on every border by enemies ready to destroy us. Things were much worse then, but he said it best: "They that can give up essential liberty to obtain a little temporary safety deserve neither liberty nor safety."

9

Mandatory School Uniforms Will Prevent Gang Violence

Al Valdez

With a master's degree in law and criminal justice and a doctorate in psychology, Al Valdez has over twenty-seven years of law enforcement experience and is currently the supervisor of the Gang Unit for the Orange County, California, district attorney's office.

Clothing is an important element of the gang subculture; certain colors and styles often act as signs of affiliation or as challenges to other gang members. As a result, innocent people unwittingly wearing gang-style clothing have been attacked and sometimes killed. School uniforms can help prevent this type of gang violence from happening at schools. When school uniforms are mandatory, students who are gang members no longer stand out as different, and their clothing no longer intimidates other students. In addition, students who look neater tend to feel more self-confident and perform better in school. When they are busy enjoying school, students are less likely to get involved in gangs.

The stylized gang attire once only worn by gang members has become a popular dress fashion worn by many young people. What many parents, teachers and young people do not understand is fashionable clothing may also be unique gang attire. Gang clothing is a gang uniform to real gang members. This stylized dress sends out a particular message to the student gang member. That is, based on the way you are dressed you have to be a gang member or associated with a gang. Some stylized clothing that is commonly worn by gang members if worn by students can make them targets for gang violence.

The student gang member is compelled to contact the student based on the way he or she dresses to determine whether or not that student is a threat or a friend to his gang. Understanding gang customs and practices becomes paramount when considering school safety issues.

Gangs Use Clothing as Signals

In the gang sub-culture clothing can act as a form of greeting, challenge or intimidation to another gang member. Young people emulating this dress style silently advertise an affiliation to a gang whether or not they really are gang associates or members. Naturally and logically real gang members will respond to this silent signal. This can happen on and off campus and at school sponsored events.

One way to minimize the impact of gang clothing has been the use of school uniforms.

There are many documented instances where non-gang member students inadvertently wearing a certain color or style of clothing have been targeted and attacked by gang members, sometimes receiving fatal injuries. Gang members key in on the style and the color of dress other people are wearing. Remember, stylized clothing can be a gang signal, a recognizable gang uniform. Many innocent citizens have been killed because they were mistakenly identified as a gang member by other gang members, based on clothing.

School Uniforms Help Students Learn

Many students and teachers become street savvy and understand the meanings of color and gang clothing. One way to minimize the impact of gang clothing has been the use of school uniforms. School uniforms can offer positive reinforcement to the students. Uniforms can help build greater self-esteem. When wearing school uniforms gang member students do not stand out as being different. The gang attire can no longer function as a silent way of claiming gang membership, acting as a greeting, challenge or intimidation.

As outward appearances become less of a factor, self-consciousness decreases and self-confidence tends to increase. The students also simply look neater and tend to feel better about themselves. Remember, these changes may take some time. Anecdotal evidence that tends to support this comes from the military. What happens to young men and women in boot camp?

Secondly, it is well established that students do not learn well when scared. Gang clothing can cause fear, intimidation and uneasiness especially when recognized by the students. Uniforms can take away this gang signal. Uniforms can help take away the real or perceived intimidation and threats caused by gang style clothing. The classroom becomes and feels safer and the students can focus their attention on learning. Teachers tend to become more relaxed and can focus their attentions on teaching.

The school uniform also becomes representative of the school. Students who dress to learn will learn, youth that dress for play will play. The concept is simple, just like kids' attitudes and behaviors change when wearing Cub Scout, Girl Scout, or sports uniforms. These uniforms send out clear and specific messages to those who wear them and are easily recognizable by those who are familiar with them.

The uniforms have a couple of additional effects. People who do not belong at school or on campus are easier to identify. These non-students will stand out in the school setting. Obviously, this would aid school administrators and staff to keep the campus safe by keeping unwanted non-students off campus.

The other unique benefit also happens within the classroom. I have spoken to a number of teachers who like the fact that all the students within their classrooms are equal. Gang members can no longer intimidate other students and teachers through dress style. Teachers have commented that it has become easier to teach because no particular student(s) stand out. If the teacher is more comfortable, the better job of teaching he or she can do.

It follows that if students feel better about themselves, they will feel better about attending school. The school can become a safe haven for the children and they will want to be there. When children are consistently in school they will be more likely to work. School attendance can and will increase and become constant.

Naturally, if students come to school on a regular basis, their grades are bound to improve. When students do not have to worry about school safety or about what they are wearing, it gives them more time to concentrate on their studies. Overall scholastic performance will tend to increase for the school.

School Uniforms Can Prevent Juvenile Crime

It also follows that students who enjoy school will also tend to participate in extracurricular activities. They will stay busy and are less likely to get in trouble. There will no longer be any competition for designer sports logo clothing or brand name clothing. For the most part, youth who are busy are more likely able to stay out of trouble and less likely to join street gangs. This suggests that juvenile crime should decrease on and off campus and the impact of the gang can be decreased if not minimized.

With the breaking down of the stand out barrier a school tends to become more unified. The students and parents identify with the school. Education becomes a motivating partnership between the school, the student and parents. With this partnership comes greater school pride and better student behavior. Students can develop a sense of unity and identity with the school. The school becomes a supplemental and in some cases a primary source for that sense of belonging. Choosing styles and color of clothing used to be only a matter of fashion and taste. Unfortunately, today it can be a matter of life and death for students and teachers.

Students who dress to learn will learn . . . and those who dress to gang bang will gang bang.

Dress Codes Lessen Gang Influence

Along the same line as school uniforms are school dress codes. There are those who feel school uniforms would be an infringement of the First Amendment right to freedom of expression. Remember students who dress to learn will learn, just like youth who dress in football uniforms play football, and those who dress to gang bang will gang bang. In today's world, gang style clothing can be a distraction to students, teachers and other gang members in and outside the classroom. Strict dress codes are yet another way to control the impact of gang attire and influence on campus.

Dress codes can take away the gangs' silent advertisement of affiliation or membership on school campuses. The only focus is to make the school a safer place to learn, not to restrict the style of dress one wears out of school. School uniforms and strict dress codes are both effective ways of managing the gang presence at school. School uniforms and strict dress codes can help make the school campus a neutral zone for all. This neutral zone is for all students, teachers and staff. This implies that schools can become a safe zone for education. In most states, schools are authorized by law to control dress styles worn by students while at school.

10

Community Involvement Will Curtail Gang Violence

Stephanie L. Mann

Stephanie L. Mann has been a safety and violence prevention consultant for more than thirty years. She is the author of Street Safe Kids and Teens.

Crime and violence, especially among young people, are serious problems for America; however, there are many effective ways for communities to organize to prevent crime. For example, neighbors can set up a network of communication and become informed about what is happening in the neighborhood.

Communities can thereby become aware of neglected or abused children and can provide role models and emotional support for those children who might otherwise turn to gangs. Also, when residents develop community crime prevention programs, they can be the "eyes and ears" for the police and alert local law enforcement of illegal activities such as drug deals, thefts, and gang crimes. Community involvement is a powerful tool in keeping neighborhoods safe.

Crime and violence create dangerous streets that are roadblocks to economic and community revitalization. When community leaders and neighbors work together and focus on community involvement, crime is reduced and citizens prevent new crimes from occurring. Involvement works and it is cost effective!

An involved community has the power to stop violent behavior, which is an ongoing problem. A January 5, 1996 report

Stephanie L. Mann, "Creating Peace," Community Peacemakers and Walkabouts for Peace, April 18, 2005. Reproduced by permission.

by the Council on Crime in America stated, "America is a ticking violent crime bomb, and there is little time remaining to prepare for the blast."

Children are the largest group of crime victims and victimizers. Bullying starts at an early age and can be fueled by frustration and anger. In Richmond, CA a six-year-old was charged with burglary and attempted murder of a month-old baby. Neighbors knew he was a neglected child but failed to seek help. Without parental guidance or community support, children fend for themselves. Unchecked bully behavior can escalate while victims of bullies may join gangs (300,000 gang members in CA) for protection, and vandalize, steal, destroy property and even commit murder. The peak age for burglary is 16 years old and the peak age for violent criminal behavior is 18.

Community Cooperation

The breakdown of the family and social isolation contributes to violent behavior. It costs $48,000 per year to lock up juveniles. The California Youth Authority is in crisis with a 91 percent recidivism rate. The *San Francisco Chronicle* (2/11/04) states, "Juvenile justice system called breeding ground for thuggery" and "Violence is 'out of control' in state's juvenile facilities."

Organized neighbors prevent crime from happening in the first place.

Local politicians can help solve the problem by speaking up about individual responsibility at the community level. Community leaders, citizens and politicians must work together to make involvement a top priority issue. Trust and understanding grows as people work together to solve problems.

Cities respond to crime by hiring more police. Of course we need adequate police protection but police are trained to react to crime. The national average is 2.7 police for every 1000 citizens with an average cost of $ 90,000 annually per officer including a patrol car. Police have been promoting "Neighborhood Watch" for 20 years. Residents are asked to be the "eyes and ears" for the police, report suspicious activities and lock up their homes. Police efforts are an important step but results can be spotty, fragmented and often temporary. . . .

Organized neighbors prevent crime from happening in the first place. Community leaders can promote and help residents take responsibility for their own safety. In some areas, it may require funding trainers to restore a network of community support. Trainers can change behavior from dependency to responsibility. Citizens need to understand their role in community building if we are going to keep children safe.

Neighborhood Communication

Most crimes are invisible. When neighbors know each other and set up a network of communication via computer or "phone tree," they stay informed. To stop juvenile crime, adults must hold juveniles accountable before problems get out of control. Neighbors can support parents and keep small problems from escalating into criminal behavior.

Organized neighbors reduce social isolation that contributes to domestic abuse (1 in 4 women are in abusive relationships). Children are often disconnected from family, neighbors and community support. At-risk children often feel powerless. If no one cares, a child learns to stop caring about other people. This environment can set up a pattern of destructive behavior.

Neighbors who know each other become aware of neglected and abused children. They can reach out or ask child protective services for assistance. A religious organization could be asked to help because they offer emotional support, mentors and role models. Citizen leadership can spread the responsibility for a family's welfare to the larger community.

Neighborhood Organization

To focus on community responsibility for children, a citywide program can be broken down into districts. Each district can establish a child safety committee. Committee members can network with city agencies and organize around a variety of concerns:

- Find mentors for at-risk children

- Appoint a teen court

- Promote mediation training

- Offer parent and youth education

- Sponsor youth-led projects

- Promote neighborhood improvement

- Offer team building training

- Encourage student safety committees

- Collaborate with businesses to create drug-free workplaces and underage access to alcohol and tobacco.

City leaders can establish training programs for "community coaches" and hire responsible residents right out of troubled neighborhoods. Just as a football coach learns skills to develop his winning football team, a "community coach" develops teamwork so neighbors can take charge of neighborhood safety.

Organized groups across the country have worked with police to stop burglaries, graffiti, drug dealers, thefts, and gangs.

Coaches can network with block associations, tenant councils, schools, businesses and local religious organizations. In most cities, there are religious organizations on every other corner. If members of a congregation reached out to neighbors they might sponsor a block party, help clean up the neighborhood, publish a neighborhood newsletter or create a community garden. Everyone benefits when people help each other.

Education empowers citizens and reduces fear. The FBI Uniform Crime Report states, 90 percent of all crimes are against property, not people. Most crimes are "crimes of opportunity," entering homes through unlocked doors or windows. Parents can help protect children if they know what to do and how to do it. . . .

Every neighborhood has potential leaders. Organized groups across the country have worked with police to stop burglaries, graffiti, drug dealers, thefts, and gangs. Citizens have recorded illegal activities, set up patrols and shut down crack houses.

Getting communities organized should be top priority! Education and communication are critical to the safety and protection of children. Every juvenile delinquent, gang member, drug abuser and abused child is growing up in someone's neighborhood. When citizens stop tolerating crime and violence, our communities will be healthier and safer environments for everyone to live. . . .

Crime Prevention Success Stories

In 1969, Orinda, CA was an unincorporated community of 17,000 residents experiencing over 400 burglaries. The volunteer association president appointed a citizen's crime prevention committee to tackle the problem. The volunteers organized neighborhoods, sponsored community forums and drug education programs at the high school. Within 2 1/2 years, crimes decreased 48 percent. At that time, Orinda had 2 sheriff's deputies and no local police department.

Barbara lives in San Pablo, CA across from a park that had been taken over by drug dealers. The city council voted to fence off the park. Barbara was angry because she wanted the park open for children and seniors. She went door to door organizing an informal citizen's patrol. They worked with the police taking down descriptions, documenting drug deals and became a visible presence. Within 3 1/2 months residents took back the park. Neighbors went to the city council requesting the money for the fence to be used for new park benches and tables. Their request was granted.

In Richmond, CA, Abraham, a retired construction worker, saw crime increasing. He decided to take the initiative and visit every home in his area. He identified 21 block leaders who agreed to organize their neighborhoods. The word got out to vandals, burglars and thieves, and crime decreased dramatically within a month. . . .

In East Oakland CA, Jossi Jones was out of work. She organized the Alpha Omega Foundation to help high-risk kids and the homeless in her neighborhood. Four years later, 35 kids attend her "Amazing Kids Summer Camp" and she teaches them how to take control of their lives. She also provides jobs, projects and shelter for the homeless. She has a staff, community respect and support. Jossi loves making a difference in her neighbor's lives.

11

Improving Public Education Will Help End Gang Violence

Tom Hayden

A former state senator and assemblyman from California, Tom Hayden is an author and political activist.

One of the major reasons young people join gangs is because they have dropped out of school and are desperate to win some kind of status—even as a member of a gang. In some urban areas rife with gang activity, the drop-out rate is higher than 50 percent. To make matters worse, many public schools that are located in impoverished neighborhoods are abysmally substandard, often lacking credentialed teachers, adequate textbooks, and functional bathrooms. Faced with such dismal conditions for learning, many students—mainly disadvantaged African Americans and Latinos—do poorly in school and ultimately drop out and become involved in gang violence. Until the public schools receive adequate funding and improve their methods of teaching, gang violence will remain a problem.

School reform has received too little attention in the debate over preventing gang violence. Significant attention instead goes to identifying and removing suspected gang members from school campuses and placing them in the equivalent of reform schools with euphemisms like "opportunity schools." Too often they spend their time there adrift until the criminal justice system finally draws them in. The drop-out rates in our urban public schools are hard to estimate, often for public relations reasons, but it is probable that percentages are up to 50 percent in many poor areas. [Criminology professor at University of California–Irvine] James Diego Vigil cites a rate of 30 to 50 percent in such schools in Los Angeles, including some that are perilously higher. At Fremont High, for example, where 80 percent of the student body comes from economically disadvantaged black and Latino families, every year, two-thirds of the ninth graders leave before high school graduation. California leads the nation in numbers of children living in households headed by a high school dropout. According to UCLA's Jeannie Oakes, "poverty is most predictive of educational achievement, and poverty is concentrated in particular neighborhoods." In other words, zip code is the best predictor of school outcomes despite fifty years of "equal opportunity."

The drop-out rate in inner-city schools is both a measurement and a major cause of the persistence of the gang subculture.

Schools Force Students to Drop Out

Nationally, the drop-out rate among immigrant Latinos between ages sixteen and nineteen was 34 percent. A Johns Hopkins [University] study described 300 high schools as "drop-out factories," while Presidents [Bill] Clinton and [George W.] Bush rattled on about "leaving no child behind." In 2003, the gross failure to report accurate drop-out rates mushroomed into a scandal at the Houston school district once celebrated by President George Bush as "the Texas miracle." Instead of meeting the president's pledge of leaving no child behind, the Houston district was disguising the attrition of thousands of at-risk students through "Enron accounting" techniques [i.e., fudging the books to make the bottom line look better than it was], according to a district staff member. The dirty secrets were revealed also in a *New York Times* report that accused the school district of creating thousands of "pushouts" in order to raise academic standards. One advocate described frightened guidance counselors "calling on their cell phones from bathrooms saying they've been told to get rid of kids."

Ominously for the future, census data showed the number of children living in poverty during the gilded nineties remained "virtually unchanged." The largest immigration wave in American history is doubling the number of students with limited English skills, and straining states like North Carolina, Nebraska, Tennessee, and Georgia without an existing capacity for bilingual or English-as-a-second-language classes.

The drop-out rate in inner-city schools is both a measurement and a major cause of the persistence of the gang subculture. As Vigil's work concludes, "What is important to note is that school problems generally precede and contribute to involvement in the gang. Thus, if only we could find effective ways to turn students on to the benefits and values of an education, the educational system could be a powerful factor in preventing students from joining gangs." Of course, numerous gang members attend and even complete school, but in general the gang subculture is a drop-out subculture. Abandoning or being driven out of school is a definitive moment after which a gang identity becomes more important. Already plagued by feelings of inferiority, these dropouts are bombarded with the message that a college education is necessary to a middle-class life. They don't need math to know from an early age that the goal of a college education has become less affordable as they grow up, even if they beat the odds and succeed in school. And the failure of the civil rights movement is apparent in the resegregation of the nation's schools which has worsened in their lifetimes. . . .

Schools Are Not Created Equal

In 1999, with a team of civil rights advocates and UCLA educational reformers, I tried to legislate disclosure of resource inequalities in schools across the state, with the goal of establishing basic standards assuring all students the equal "opportunity to learn," which by then was the modified goal of the equal opportunity movement. The [California governor] Gray Davis administration, like many in the national education establishment, was threatened by the prospect of information about school disparities becoming public, and vetoed the bill. But the lawsuits by the ACLU [American Civil Liberties Union] went forward, with findings that were shocking. Often, students in inner-city schools lacked desks at which to sit, and instead perched on counters in their classes. Some classes lacked any teachers at all, but instead were void for weeks at a time or were filled by permanent substitutes. Without classes to attend, students were channeled into "service" classes two periods each day, where they were allowed to run errands or sit on the floor. Most students had no books to take home. In one math class, students waited an entire semester before receiving books. Students were forced to pay for their own education materials, including test primers. The multitrack system meant that students received twenty fewer days of instruction yearly than students in schools without multitrack years. At one school with more than 3,500 students in Los Angeles, there were only two functioning bathrooms each for boys and girls, with stall doors broken open and missing soap and toilet paper. There was just one college counselor for the same school's student body. As the lawsuit charged, "experts have found that student achievement falls as many as 11 percentile points in schools with substandard building conditions . . . [and] the difference between an effective and an ineffective teacher can be a full grade level of student achievement in a year. . . . *Repeated deprivation of basic learning tools continues to create learning deficits from which children can never recover.*" Only 3 percent of students at some of these "educational slums" were proficient readers, while the statewide achievement gap between poor and affluent schools in reading and math widened in every grade between 1997 and 2002. . . .

Studies . . . have shown minority youth to be at higher risk of punishment than whites who have committed the same delinquent behavior.

"Unsalvageable Troublemakers"

In her 2001 study *Bad Boys: Public Schools in the Making of Black Masculinity*, Smith College professor Ann Arnett Ferguson has demonstrated how at-risk African American students, classified as "unsalvageable troublemakers" in their school setting, "recoup a sense of self as competent and worthy under extremely discouraging work conditions. Sadly, they do this by getting in trouble." These young men respond with "attitude" when expected to perform with the "absolute docility that goes against the grain of masculinity," Ferguson found. They identify with blackness (or, for Latino boys, chicanismo) in the face of a school system that denies the existence of racism. In doing so, they refashion themselves to "recoup personal esteem" in a manner that subverts white authority, if only unconsciously. They fight both ritually, for respect and to avoid being picked on later in a middle-class, *kumbaya* [i.e., a falsely warm and friendly] setting where disputes are supposed to be "talked out." They become involved in what [educator and author] Herbert Kohl describes as "active not-learning," expending their intelligence and energy in distancing themselves from their schoolwork because, as he describes it,

> "To agree to learn from a stranger who does not respect your integrity causes a major loss of self. The only alternative is to not-learn and reject the stranger's world."

Another insightful researcher, L. Jannelle Dance, has described how this oppositional behavior is seen by those in authority as dangerously gang-related. Like most careful observers, Dance knows that "only a small minority of urban youths are actually involved in hardcore criminal activities." But they adopt a "tough front" in the form of "gangsterlike mannerisms, language and dispositions," most often temporarily as a strategy for navigating and surviving the streets. Such youth are classified as troublemakers for behavior that might be tolerated among white youth, but is unacceptably threatening when coming from youth of color. Ferguson notes studies that have shown minority youth to be at higher risk of punishment than whites who have committed the same delinquent behavior. When disciplined, the youth she observed were sent to an isolated room, which, significantly, they called "the dungeon" or "the prison," where their newly born "bad" reputations were further reinforced. The alternative, that *schools might be designed to lessen alienation or shame,* is beyond the imagination of many administrators, teachers, parents, and public officials who are more likely to support even sterner academic "boot camps." In 2002, the Philadelphia school district suspended thirty-three *kindergartners* for punching teachers and stabbing one another with pencils. . . .

Gang members felt that knowledge was a mystical sacrament they had been denied.

Innovative Programs for At-Risk Students

Glaring examples of the dominant culture are police-based classroom programs such as Drug Abuse Resistance Education (DARE) and the federally supported Gang Resistance Education and Training Program (GREAT). Though little evidence exists that DARE accomplishes its purported goals, the program is widely entrenched nationally. In 2000, the California legislature succeeded in preventing a subsidy of $1 million in public funds annually for DARE. GREAT is a newer program, taught by police with little involvement of teachers, whose stated goals are to reduce gang membership, prevent crime and violence, and develop positive attitudes toward law enforcement. Since the youth drawn toward gangs carry more antisocial beliefs than mainstream students, a police officer forcefully demanding respect is likely to have little impact. Studies showed a relatively unfavorable effect among students two years after attending the classes, followed by modest success four years later as many students matured. GREAT had virtually no effect on the cohort of students who dropped out or were highly marginal. . . .

Innovative research on the potential of successfully educating gang members has been done by researchers like David Brotherton at the John Jay College of Criminal Justice in Manhattan, whose team has been doing innovative street research with the Latin Kings [gang] for several years. Brotherton points out that most gang research assumes that gang members reject schooling or are flatly uneducable, instead of asking whether schools as institutions are designed to reject gang members. In interviews with the Latin Kings and the Asociación Neta from 1997 to 2000, however, Brotherton found a strong belief in the empowering function of education. These gang members felt that knowledge was a mystical sacrament they had been denied. Knowledge, Brotherton heard over and over, was the key to self-improvement, cultural identity, and overcoming barriers. Internally, education—learning Puerto Rican history, studying King manifestos, teachings, and by-laws—was a means of advancing within the organization. Externally, education meant advancing the next generation of "little homies" and being able to relate to the mass media, politicians, and potential allies. Brotherton found that many local Kings placed a priority on checking school attendance records of the peewees, enforced their own 10 P.M. curfews on youths under sixteen, engaged in counseling those in trouble, and tried to steer younger members out of needless conflicts. "Our goal is to strive for more knowledge, more kids, more of our brothers goin' into schools without being kicked out for being a King. Becoming lawyers, doctors, cops, becoming all these things we're striving for . . ."

At-Risk Students Need a Different Curriculum

In notes on "a pedagogy of possibility," Brotherton stressed the critical role of schools in the inner city. Based on his interviews and experiences, he summarized the following:

- Gang students want to be mentored. They want attention, and crave to be valued other than in street guises.

- Gang students have hope. Many see their gang experience as transitional; all spoke of wanting to leave at some point.

- Gang members are expressive, with a flair for artistic imagery and poetry.

- Gang students are very interested in their ethnic culture.

- Gang students are communal and collective; they hate the competition and favoritism in typical school culture but are open to learning together.

I would argue that homies exhibit a *mischanneled* intelligence, not a hopeless deficiency. Like people who know baseball averages but can't understand mathematics, homies are frequently brilliant in video arcades but can't function in a classroom. They invent complicated hand signs, tattoos, and graffiti symbols but often read at third-grade levels. It is not creativity that is lacking so much as a setting for intelligence to flourish. As Brotherton puts it, "In a more humane and reasonable world, we would have an enormous amount to learn from these groups' efforts to organize the disenfranchised and underserved populations," citing three specific possibilities: first, public schools could learn how groups such as the Kings build self-esteem; second, the schools could study the ways the Kings develop leadership skills and bonds of loyalty among youth who drop out of conventional structures; and third, schools could learn from the curriculum that such groups develop, inevitably stressing new interpretations of colonial history, the dynamics of oppression, and the role of spiritual and intellectual resistance to assaults on identity.

Schools remain contestable sites in the struggle to ensure a better future for gang members and all at-risk youth. But will policymakers and teachers be committed to the challenge? As long as the war on gangs continues, how many Americans will support increased resources to educating those who are demonized as an incorrigible enemy?

Organizations to Contact

American Civil Liberties Union (ACLU)
125 Broad St., 18th Fl., New York, NY   10004
(212) 549-2500 • fax: (212) 549-2646
e-mail: aclu@aclu.org
Web site: www.aclu.org

The ACLU is a national organization that works to defend Americans' civil rights as guaranteed by the U.S. Constitution. It opposes curfew laws for juveniles and others and seeks to protect the public-assembly rights of gang members or people associated with gangs. The ACLU publishes the biannual newsletter *Civil Liberties*.

Boys and Girls Clubs of America
1275 Peachtree St. NE, Atlanta, GA   30309-3506
(404) 487-5700
e-mail: info@bgca.org
Web site: www.bgca.org

Boys and Girls Clubs of America supports juvenile gang prevention programs in its individual clubs throughout the United States. The organization's Targeted Outreach Delinquency Prevention program relies on referrals from schools, courts, law enforcement, and youth service agencies to recruit at-risk youths into ongoing club programs and activities. The organization publishes *Gang Prevention Through Targeted Outreach*, a manual designed to assist local clubs in reaching youngsters before they become involved in gang activity.

Center for the Study and Prevention of Violence (CSPV)
Institute of Behavioral Science, Boulder, CO   80309-0439
(303) 492-8465 • fax: (303) 443-3297
e-mail: cspv@colorado.edu
Web site: www.colorado.edu/cspv

The CSPV was founded in 1992 to provide information and assistance to organizations that are dedicated to preventing violence—particularly youth violence. Its publications include the paper "Gangs and Adolescent Violence" and the fact sheets "Gangs and Youth Violence" and "Female Juvenile Violence."

Child Welfare League of America (CWLA)
440 First St. NW, 3rd Fl., Washington, DC   20001-2085
(202) 638-2952 • fax: (202) 638-4004
Web site: www.cwla.org

The Child Welfare League of America, a social welfare organization concerned with setting standards for welfare and human services agencies, works to improve care and services for abused, dependent, or neglected children, youth, and their families. It publishes information on gangs and youth crime in the bimonthly journal *Child Welfare* as well as in several books, including *Beating the Odds: Crime, Poverty, and Life in the Inner City* and *Girls in the Juvenile Justice System*.

Gang Awareness Training Education (GATE)
410 Cardinal Dr., Bartlett, IL   60103
(630) 973-0235
e-mail: info@openthegate.org
Web site: www.openthegate.org

GATE is a school-based antigang education program for young people. Taught by local police officers, the GATE program focuses on reducing the gang presence in and around communities and schools.

National Council on Crime and Delinquency (NCCD)
1970 Broadway, Suite 500, Oakland, CA   94612
(510) 208-0500 • fax: (510) 208-0511
Web site: www.nccd-crc.org

The NCCD assists government, law enforcement, and community organizations in developing programs to address juvenile justice and gang problems. It conducts research, promotes reform initiatives, and works to prevent and reduce juvenile crime and delinquency. The council publishes the informational booklet *Reducing Crime in America: A Pragmatic Approach.*

National Crime Prevention Council (NCPC)
1000 Connecticut Ave. NW, 13th Fl., Washington, DC   20036
(202) 466-6272 • fax: (202) 296-1356
Web site: www.ncpc.org

The council works to prevent juvenile crime and to build safer neighborhoods. Its Youth as Resources program, which encourages local youngsters to implement projects to help their communities, is based on the premise that young people have the desire and capability to address many youth crime problems on their own. The council's publications include two informational packets: *Helping Youth with Gang Prevention* and *Tools to Involve Parents in Gang Prevention.*

National Gang Crime Research Center (NGCRC)
PO Box 990, Peotone, IL   60468-0990
(708) 258-9111 • fax: (708) 258-9546
e-mail: gangcrime@aol.com
Web site: www.ngcrc.com

The NGCRC is a nonprofit, independent agency that conducts research on gangs and gang members and disseminates information through publications and reports. It publishes the *Journal of Gang Research.*

National Major Gang Task Force (NMGTF)
338 S. Arlington Ave., Suite 112, Indianapolis, IN   46219
(317) 322-0537 • fax: (317) 322-0549
e-mail: nmgtf@earthlink.net
Web site: www.nmgtf.org

The NMGTF's goal is to provide a centralized link for all fifty state correctional systems, the Federal Bureau of Prisons, major jails, law enforcement officers, and probation and parole officers throughout the nation. The task force accomplishes this mission by generating and maintaining the National Correction Informational Sharing System, which is available to gang prevention groups across the country. It publishes the monograph "From the Street to the Prison: Understanding and Responding to Gangs."

National School Safety Center (NSSC)
141 Duesenberg Dr., Suite 11, Westlake Village, CA   91362
(805) 373-9977 • fax: (805) 373-9277
Web site: www.nssc1.org

Part of Pepperdine University, the center is a research organization that studies school crime and violence, including gang and hate crimes, and provides technical assistance to local school systems. NSSC believes that teacher training is an effective means of reducing these problems. Its publications include the book *Gangs in Schools: Breaking Up Is Hard to Do* and the handout "Working Together to Create Safe Schools."

National Youth Gang Center (NYGC)
Institute for Intergovernmental Research
Tallahassee, FL   32317
(850) 385-0600 • fax: (850) 386-5356
e-mail: nygc@iir.com
Web site: www.iir.com/nygc

The National Youth Gang Center was developed by the Office of Juvenile Justice and Delinquency Prevention (OJJDP) to collect, analyze, and distribute information on gangs and gang-related legislation, research, and programs. Its publications include *The NYGC Bibliography of Gang Literature*. It also makes numerous gang-related articles accessible on its Web site and on *OJJDP's Gang Publication,* a CD-ROM that it distributes on request.

National Youth Violence Prevention Resource Center (NYVPRC)
PO Box 10809, Rockville, MD   20849-0809

(866) 723-3968 • fax: (301) 562-1001
e-mail: nyvprc@safeyouth.org
Web site: www.safeyouth.org

The National Youth Violence Prevention Resource Center serves as a point of access to current information developed by federal agencies or with federal support pertaining to youth violence. The center offers the latest tools to facilitate discussion with children, to resolve conflicts nonviolently, and to end violence committed by and against young people. Its publications include the fact sheets "Youth Gangs" and "A Parent's Quick Reference Card: Recognizing and Preventing Gang Involvement."

**Office of Juvenile Justice and
Delinquency Prevention (OJJDP)**
810 Seventh St. NW, Washington, DC   20531
(202) 307-5911 • fax: (202) 307-2093
Web site: www.ojjdp.ncjrs.org

As the primary federal agency charged with monitoring and improving the juvenile justice system, the OJJDP develops and funds programs on juvenile justice. Through its Juvenile Justice Clearinghouse, the OJJDP distributes fact sheets, the annual *National Youth Gang Survey*, and reports such as "Youth Gangs: An Overview" and "Gang Suppression and Intervention: Community Models."

Teens Against Gang Violence (TAGV)
1486 Dorchester Ave., Dorchester, MA   02124
(617) 825-8248
e-mail: teensagv@aol.com
Web site: www.tagv.org

Teens Against Gang Violence is a volunteer, community-based, teen peer leadership program. Through presentations and workshops, the organization educates teens, parents, schools, and community groups on violence, guns, and drug prevention. It provides information about its programs on its Web site.

Bibliography

Books

Lawrence Balter and Catherine S. Tamis-Lemonda, eds. *Child Psychology: A Handbook of Contemporary Issues.* New York: Psychology Press, 2003.

Caroline S. Clauss-Ehlers and Mark D. Weist, eds. *Community Planning to Foster Resilience in Children.* New York: Kluwer Academic/Plenum, 2004.

G. David Curry and Scott Decker *Confronting Gangs: Crime and Community.* 2nd ed. Los Angeles: Roxbury, 2003.

Scott Decker *Policing Gangs and Youth Violence.* Belmont, CA: Wadsworth, 2002.

Elizabeth Kandel Englander *Understanding Violence.* Mahwah, NJ: Lawrence Erlbaum Associates, 2003.

R. Barri Flowers *Kids Who Commit Adult Crimes: Serious Criminality by Juvenile Offenders.* Binghamton, NY: Haworth, 2002.

Celeste Fremon *G-dog and the Homeboys: Father Greg Boyle and the Gangs of East Los Angeles.* Albuquerque: University of New Mexico Press, 2004.

Sharon H. Grant and Richard Van Acker *Challenges of Gangs and Youth Violence in Schools.* Arlington, VA: Council for Exceptional Children, 2002.

Tom Hayden   *Street Wars: Gangs and the Future of Violence*. New York: New Press, 2006.

James C. Howell   *Preventing and Reducing Juvenile Delinquency: A Comprehensive Framework*. Thousand Oaks, CA: Sage, 2003.

C. Ronald Huff   *Gangs in America III*. Thousand Oaks, CA: Sage, 2002.

Malcolm W. Klein   *Gang Cop: The Words and Ways of Officer Paco Domingo*. Lanham, MD: Alta Mira, 2004.

Louis Kontos, David C. Brotherton, and Luis Barrios, eds.   *Gangs and Society*. New York: Columbia University Press, 2003.

Jose M. Lopez   *Gangs: Casualties in an Undeclared War*. Dubuque, IA: Kendall Hunt, 2002.

John Muncie   *Youth and Crime*. Thousand Oaks, CA: Sage, 2004.

Rebecca D. Petersen   *Understanding Contemporary Gangs in America: An Interdisciplinary Approach*. Upper Saddle River, NJ: Prentice Hall, 2003.

Michael Scott   *Lords of Lawndale: My Life in a Chicago White Street Gang*. Bloomington, IN: Authorhouse, 2004.

James Short and Lorine A. Hughes, eds.   *Studying Youth Gangs*. Lanham, MD: Alta Mira, 2006.

Colton Simpson
and Ann
Pearlman

*Inside the Crips: Life Inside L.A.'s
Most Notorious Gang.* New York: St.
Martin's, 2005.

Terence P.
Thornberry,
Marvin D. Krohn,
et al.

*Gangs and Delinquency in Develop-
mental Perspective.* New York: Cam-
bridge University Press, 2003.

Michael Ungar,
ed.

*Handbook for Working with Children
and Youth: Pathways to Resilience
Across Cultures and Contexts.* Thousand Oaks, CA: Sage, 2005.

Al Valdez

*Gangs: A Guide to Understanding
Street Gangs.* 4th ed. San Clemente,
CA: Law Tech, 2005.

James Diego Vigil

*A Rainbow of Gangs: Street Cultures
in the Mega-City.* Austin: University
of Texas Press, 2002.

Terrell C. Wright

Home of the Body Bags. Los Angeles:
SenegalPress, 2005.

Periodicals

Beth Barrett and
Phillip W. Browne

"Search for Solutions That Last," *Los
Angeles Daily News*, September 28,
2004.

Amy Benfer

"Policing Gangsta Fashion: Are 'Anti-gang' Dress Codes in Malls a Way to Deter Crime, or Just Another Way to Prosecute Patrons for Shopping While Black?" Salon.com, May 29, 2002.

Kevin Butler

"Reaching out to Troubled Youths," *Los Angeles Daily News*, October 1, 2004.

Arian Campo-Flores

"The Most Dangerous Gang in America; They're a Violent Force in 33 States and Counting. Inside the Battle to Police Mara Salvatrucha. (MS-13 Is a Gang Growing in Strength in the United States)," *Newsweek*, March 28, 2005.

CBS News

"Feds Nab 375 Gang Members," March 10, 2006. www.cbsnews.com/.

Christian Science Monitor

"As Gangs Rise, So Do Calls for U.S.-Wide Dragnet," February 4, 2004.

CNN.com

"Feds Target Gangs in Crackdown," March 11, 2006. www.cnn.com/.

David Crary

"Gang Violence: A Federal Crime?" CBS News, May 9, 2005. www.cbsnews.com/.

Donna DeCesare   "Dangerous Exile: More than 400,000
                    Noncitizens Have Been Deported
                    Since 1996 Because of Expanded
                    Criminal Sentences. A Photojournal-
                    ist Follows the Return of Central
                    American and Caribbean Deportees,"
                    Colorlines, Fall 2003.

Scott H. Decker   "Young Women and Gang Violence:
                    Gender, Street Offending, and Violent
                    Victimization in Gangs," *Justice
                    Quarterly*, March 31, 2001.

Daniel Duane   "Straight Outta Boston: Why Is the
                    'Boston Miracle'—the Only Tactic
                    Proven to Reduce Gang Violence—
                    Being Dissed by the L.A.P.D., the
                    FBI, and Congress?" *Mother Jones*,
                    January/February 2006.

Thomas   "In a One-Room School, a Tough
Fields-Meyer   Teacher Makes Miracles: After Losing
                    One Student to Gang Violence, Paul
                    White Vowed to Save Other Kids. By
                    Showing Teens from L.A.'s Meanest
                    Streets They Have a Future, He's Suc-
                    ceeding," *People*, May 16, 2005.

Paul J. Fink   "Counteracting Gang Violence,"
                    Clinical Psychiatry News, July 1, 2004.

William Flores   "Gang Truce Worked, Could Again,"
and Patricia   *Los Angeles Daily News*, August 15,
O'Donnell   2002.
Brummett

Hector Gonzalez   "Why Gang Intervention Doesn't Work," *Silicon Valley De-Bug*, July 27, 2005. www.siliconvalleydebug.com/.

Melody Griffin and Mike Meacham   "Gangs in Schools: An Introduction to the Problem and Interventions," *Annals of the American Psychotherapy Association*, 2002.

Jennifer Hojaiban   "Gang Bill Would Expand 'Crime of Violence' Definition and Otherwise Negatively Impact Noncitizens," *Immigrants' Rights Update*, October 5, 2005.

Iris Kuo   "Deportation the Latest Weapon Against Gang Violence," *San Jose (CA) Mercury News*, March 10, 2006.

Erik K. Laursen   "Rather than Fixing Kids—Build Positive Peer Cultures," *Reclaiming Children and Youth*, Fall 2005.

Marcy Levin-Epstein   "Rise in Gang Activity Suspected," *Inside School Safety*, January 2004.

Robert J. Lopez, Rich Connell, and Chris Kraul   "MS-13: An International Franchise: Gang Uses Deportation to Its Advantage to Flourish in U.S.," *Los Angeles Times*, October 30, 2005.

David Madrid   "Like It or Not, Gangs Are San Jose's Social Movements," *Silicon Valley De-Bug*, June 22, 2005. www.siliconvalley debug.com/.

David Madrid   "To Keep Kids out of Gangs, Give
                      Them Identity," *Pacific News Service*,
                      June 21, 2005. http://news.pacific
                      news.org/.

Terry McCarthy   "The Gang Buster: Bratton Cut
                      Crime in New York, and Now He's
                      Doing It in L.A. His Secret: Giving
                      Cops More Power," *Time*, January 19,
                      2004.

Robert Morales   "A Narrow Escape from Life in
                      Gang," *Los Angeles Daily News*, Sep-
                      tember 26, 2004.

Askia Muhammad   "Deadly Silence Covers Passing of
                      Federal Gang Bill: Federal Gang-
                      busters Bill Legitimizes Sinister Mea-
                      sures," FinalCall.com News, June 2,
                      2005. www.finalcall.com/.

Nisa Islam   "Federal Gang Bill Is 'Open Warfare,'
Muhammad and   Says Activist," FinalCall.com News,
Saeed Shabazz   September 10, 2004. www.finalcall
                      .com/.

Judy Muller   "Gang Violence Surges in L.A.," ABC
                      News, March 30, 2006. www.abcnews
                      .com/.

PAHO Today   "Gang Violence Requires a Preventive
                      Approach," April 3, 2005. www.paho
                      .org/.

Mark Preston   "Taking Aim at Gangs," *American
                      City & County*, July 1, 2005.

Sudarsan Raghavan, Karin Brulliard, and Fulvio Cativo	"Branded in a World of Gang Warfare," *Washington Post*, August 22, 2005.
USA Today	"Gang Bloodshed Surging in Some U.S. Cities," December 11, 2002.
Jon Ward	"Anti-gang Program Guides Children," *Washington Times*, July 14, 2004.
Jon Ward	"Schools Prepare for Teen Gangs; Police Seek Assistance from Administrators," *Washington Times*, August 19, 2004.
Phelan A. Wyrick and James C. Howell	"Strategic Risk-Based Response to Youth Gangs," *Juvenile Justice Journal*, September 2004.
Gary L. Yates	"New Thinking Can Help Defeat Gang Violence," PNN Online, January 29, 2004. www.pnnonline.org

Index